The Black A

THE MYSTERIOUS PLANET

By Jez Strickley

Published October 2025 by Obverse Books

Editors: Kara Dennison, Stuart Douglas

No form of AI has been used in the creation of this book.

Recently Published

#67: *The Edge of Destruction* by Simon Guerrier

#68: *The Happiness Patrol* by Mike Stack

#69: *Midnight* by Philip Purser-Hallard

#70: *Ascension of the Cybermen / The Timeless Children* by Ryan Bradley

#71: *The Aztecs* by Doris V Sutherland

#72: *Silence in the Library / The Forest of the Dead* by Dale Smith

#73: *Under the Lake / Before the Flood* by Ryan C Parrey and Kevin S Decker

#74: *A Christmas Carol* by Jamie Beckwith and Leslie Grace McMurtry

#75: *Silver Nemesis* by James Cooray Smith

#76: *Logopolis* by Jonathan Hay

#77: *Castrovalva* by Andrew Orton

#78: *The Devil's Chord* by Dale Smith

CONTENTS

OVERVIEW

Serial Title: *The Trial of a Time Lord* Parts One to Four, aka 'The Mysterious Planet'

Writer: Robert Holmes

Director: Nicholas Mallett

Original UK Transmission Dates: 6 September 1986 – 27 September 1986

Running Time:	Part One: 24:57
	Part Two: 24:44
	Part Three: 24:18
	Part Four: 24:20
UK Viewing Figures:	Part One: 4.9 million
	Part Two: 4.9 million
	Part Three: 3.9 million
	Part Four: 3.7 million

Regular Cast: Colin Baker (The Doctor), Nicola Bryant (Peri)

Recurring Cast: Michael Jayston (The Valeyard), Lynda Bellingham (The Inquisitor)

Guest Cast: Joan Sims (Katryca), Tony Selby (Glitz), Glen Murphy (Dibber), Tom Chadbon (Merdeen), Roger Brierley (Drathro), David Rodigan (Broken Tooth), Adam Blackwood (Balazar), Timothy Walker (Grell), Billy McColl (Humker), Sion Tudor Owen (Tandrell).

Antagonists: Drathro, The Tribe of the Free, The Valeyard

Novelisation: *Doctor Who: The Mysterious Planet* by Terrance Dicks. **The Target Doctor Who Library** #127.

Responses:

'A mystery that's not much of a mystery, a conflict that's not that compelling, and characters that overall don't leave much of an impact.'
[Mahan, 'The Mysterious Planet Review' *TARDIS Guide*, 14 April 2025]

'While not the best Robert Holmes story, it's still worth watching because it is a good story. Not a classic, and not Must-See, but very entertaining nonetheless.'
[Colin D Smith, 'Who Review: The Mysterious Planet', *www.colindsmith.com*, 1 May 2018]

SYNOPSIS

Part One

(**The Doctor** is taken out of time, depriving him of his recent memories including the whereabouts of his friend **Peri**. The Time Lords' High Council has decreed that he must face an inquiry into his conduct, to be prosecuted by **the Valeyard** before **the Inquisitor**. The evidence consists of records of the Doctor's activities collected via the TARDIS, held in the Matrix, the Time Lords' universal repository of knowledge, and replayed before the court. It begins as follows...)

The Doctor and Peri arrive on a damp world, Ravolox, which intrigues the Doctor because of the characteristics it shares with Earth. Though supposedly devastated by a solar fireball centuries before, Ravolox is now forested and inhabited. Unknowingly, the Doctor narrowly avoids being shot by interstellar conman **Glitz**, who sees him as a rival. With his colleague **Dibber**, Glitz plans to sabotage the aerial of a black light converter system, worshipped as a totem by the local Tribe of the Free. However, they learn from the Tribe's leader **Katryca** that other aliens have visited with the same aim. Katryca is therefore very unimpressed by Glitz's claim that their totem will attract another cataclysm if not destroyed.

The Doctor and Peri discover an underground complex built in the ruins of London's Marble Arch Underground station, proving that Ravolox is Earth in the distant future. Upset, Peri leaves and runs into the Tribe. The Doctor descends further into 'Marb Station', where his curiosity leads him to trip an alarm and be arrested by the inhabitants as a water thief. He meets the amiable **Balazar**, who keeps the knowledge of the past in the form of three books: Herman Melville's *Moby-Dick*, Charles Kingsley's *The Water Babies* and a description of the UK habitats of the Canada goose. Balazar and his compatriots believe that the surface of Ravolox is still an uninhabitable wasteland. Their laws decree that the Doctor must be stoned to death, and they start to carry out the sentence.

Part Two

The Doctor's execution is interrupted by 'train guards' led by **Merdeen** and his subordinate **Grell**. Their ruler, 'the Immortal' – aka **Drathro**, an L3 robot, who is powered by the black light converter system – has detected an extra person in Marb Station and sent them to cull this supernumerary 'work unit'. However, they are interrupted by Drathro itself, who summons the Doctor to its fortified 'castle' complex. It has survived there since the cataclysm, served by youths selected for their intelligence, currently the perennially squabbling **Humker** and **Tandrell**. At first Drathro mistakes the Doctor for a member of a relief mission from Andromeda; when corrected, it orders the Doctor to help fix a fault in the converter system. Drathro created the underground complex to support three **'Sleepers'** from Andromeda, and although the Sleepers are now dead the robot continues to follow its programming.

Katryca welcomes Peri to the Tribe of the Free, promising to find husbands for her. In the meantime she is imprisoned with Dibber and Glitz, who is fascinated to hear from her that the Doctor, his supposed rival, is a Time Lord. Katryca orders Glitz to be sacrificed to the converter aerial totem, but instead Glitz and Peri distract the Tribe while Dibber blows it up. They then head for the tunnels, pursued by Katryca's enforcer, **Broken Tooth**, and his followers.

Meanwhile, the Doctor has escaped Drathro's castle, pursued by a more basic **L1 robot**. Merdeen, who objects to culling workers and has been secretly sending refugees to the surface for years, lets him pass but insists he take Balazar with him. The two parties meet, trapped between Broken Tooth's tribesmen and Drathro's robot.

Part Three

Broken Tooth, one of those Merdeen has rescued previously, recognises Balazar and shoots the L1 robot. The Doctor is alarmed to learn that Dibber has blown up the aerial, and fears a destructive chain reaction. He wants to return to Drathro's castle and shut down the black light converter, but Broken Tooth insists they all return to the tribal village, where Katryca refuses to believe the Doctor's concerns. Glitz confirms that Ravolox is Earth, and explains that the relief ship Drathro expected failed because the planet has been moved from its former position. Glitz himself is from Andromeda, and hopes to recover valuable data held by the Sleepers.

Underground, Grell suspects Merdeen of treachery. Humker and Tandrell manage to reactivate the L1, which pursues the escapees. Through its sensors, Drathro learns of the existence of the Tribe of the Free, and is alarmed and angry, believing that the Doctor will use them against it. It also realises that the loss of the aerial will destroy the conversion system, ending Drathro's own existence.

While recovering the Doctor, the L1 is destroyed by the Tribe. Mistakenly believing that they have killed Drathro, they launch an attack on Marb Station, joined by Glitz and Dibber with some heavy artillery. Still needing to shut down the converter, the Doctor returns with Peri to Marb Station, where Merdeen apparently shoots him with a crossbow.

Part Four

In fact, Merdeen has shot Grell, who was about to kill him for his betrayal. The Tribe storm the castle and confront Drathro, who kills Katryca and Broken Tooth. It orders Merdeen to cull the intruders, but Merdeen resists. The Doctor tries to persuade Drathro to let him shut down the converter, which will end the robot's existence to save the human populace. If it continues, the chain reaction could supposedly destroy the galaxy or even the universe, but Drathro sees no philosophical or moral reason why others should outlive itself. Glitz and Dibber arrive, and Glitz offers to return Drathro to Andromeda in return for the Sleepers' data. Drathro agrees, and is distracted for long enough to allow the Doctor to contain the explosion. The robot is destroyed, along with the sought-after data.

While Glitz and Dibber plan to salvage the valuable aerial instead, Merdeen, Balazar, Humker, Tandrell and the other survivors from the underground join the Tribe of the Free. The Doctor wonders to Peri who moved Ravolox, and the nature of the data the Sleepers held.

(In the Doctor's present, this information has been censored at the order of the High Council, which the Valeyard insists is in the public interest. The Doctor also claims that he was asked to go to Ravolox, though he does not reveal who made the request. Meanwhile, the Valeyard has successfully agitated for the inquiry into the Doctor's activities to become a trial, in which he risks a sentence of death.[1])

---

[1] The story continues in the remainder of *The Trial of a Time Lord*, initially in Parts Five to Eight, aka 'Mindwarp'.

INTRODUCTION: RAVOLOX AND ROOTEDNESS

On a late summer's evening in 1986, **Doctor Who** returned to BBC1's Saturday teatime schedule after a break of 18 months – the then longest period off air in the show's history. The new season was comprised a single 14-part serial, *The Trial of a Time Lord* in which court evidence was presented by way of three four-part adventures, followed by a two-part conclusion. The first of these evidential outings was given the working title 'The Mysterious Planet'. Here, the Doctor and Peri become embroiled in events involving postapocalyptic communities, a powerful robot and a pair of crafty conmen intent on a hi-tech heist, set on the world of Ravolox.

This book does not focus on 'The Mysterious Planet' in terms of its narrative or production elements. Instead, it sets out a series of short, philosophical commentaries, loosely tied together in parts through the concept of place as depicted through the characters and locations in the story[2]. Of these, Ravolox in and of itself is a key locus, the curious matter of its identity catalysing questions of place and placelessness[3].

There is a certain urgency to the overall topic of place, which adds to its value as a thematic marker here. The first quarter of the 21st century has witnessed schools, workplaces and social spaces become increasingly digitised, with notions of rootedness and place, which naturally emerge out of our interactions with our

[2] A 'sense of place' is the psychological connection between individuals and locations, through which our surroundings are given meaning and value.

[3] 'Placelessness' refers to locations lacking a sense of place; liminal spaces are sometimes identified as 'placeless'.

surroundings, being reimagined. In some circles, these changes do not represent an existential shift, since 'Place and space may well have been transformed in the digital era, but they continue to **matter**.'[4] For others, however, digital media are undermining our understandings of place 'because they overwhelm us with information and images, bring into question what is real and what is fake,' and leave us with what geographer Edward Relph calls 'digital disorientation'[5]. Such is the extent of this phenomenon, Relph argues, that our sense of place can become disturbed[6].

Managing this disturbance is as much about comprehending our own role in the scale of things as it is appreciating the spaces and structures we find around us. This is where rootedness, as discussed by the French thinker Simone Weil, merits attention. Weil, a mid-20th-century writer and activist, maintains that the human soul has a variety of needs, of which 'To be rooted is perhaps the most important and least recognized' of our wants and 'one of the hardest to define'. This fundamental link to our environment is natural and emerges out of a number of conditions, including geography and social arrangements. Moreover, almost all a person's ethical, cognitive and spiritual being derives from 'the environment of which he forms a natural part.'[7] Place, therefore, is critical to our individual sense of identity. Recognising its value as a personal vector only adds to its meaning and the significance of the dangers inherent in it

---

[4] Halstead, Huw, 'Cyberplace: From Fantasies of Placelessness to Connective Emplacement', *Memory Studies*, 14(3), p563.
[5] Relph, Edward, 'Digital Disorientation and Place', *Memory Studies*, 14(3), p573.
[6] Relph, 'Digital Disorientation and Place', p576.
[7] Weil, Simone, *The Need for Roots*, p40.

becoming 'more fleeting, more conflicted, more distracted' and diminished within a veritable tangle of Wi-Fi signals, where digital arrangements of place (e.g. forums) confuse or surpass traditional physical locations[8].

With the power of place and its influence on selfhood in mind, this book is split into five chapters[9]. Chapter 1 deals with conceptions of surroundings with an emphasis on places that attract and repel. Chapter 2 builds on this thread by introducing the idea of dwelling, as understood by the German thinker Martin Heidegger.

Chapter 3 takes up Heidegger's dwelling and extends it into matters of ecological concern, with an overview of ecologism and some of its exponents. Focusing on the nature of free choice in environmental matters, Chapter 4 explores whether volition and consciousness are possible in an artificial context. Lastly, Chapter 5 raises the question of personal identity, and circles back to the concept of place and its part in shaping and grounding our sense of self.

Although these chapters are presented in sequence, they are generally self-contained enough to be read in no particular order. In fact, disrupting the order is not unlike the way we make sense of ourselves and our surroundings. As the Danish philosopher Søren Kierkegaard remarked, life is understood backwards, but it is experienced forwards[10].

---

[8] Relph, 'Digital Disorientation and Place', p576.

[9] 'Selfhood' refers to individual self-awareness and possession of a rich inner mental life.

[10] Bachmetjevas, Viktoras, 'Imaginary Construction and Lessons in Living Forward', *History of European Ideas*, 47(3), p470.

CHAPTER 1: RAVOLOX, TOPOPHILIA AND TOPOPHOBIA

Robert Holmes' final complete **Doctor Who** script contains plot elements familiar to fans of his storytelling. Namely, a brace of petty criminals out to deceive a local dignitary (*The Ribos Operation* (1978)), youths taken from their families by a mysterious alien (*The Krotons* (1968-69)) and corrupt Time Lords intent on concealing a scandal (*The Deadly Assassin* (1976)). Yet, underlying these ingredients is an altogether more subtle narrative strand. It is expressed in the worlds inhabited by the Underground Dwellers and the Tribe of the Free; it is signalled in the Doctor's and Peri's reactions to the true identity of Ravolox; and it exists in the juxtaposition of Drathro's logico-rationality and the emotional registers of Tandrell and Humker. The thread in question is topophilia: literally, 'love of place'; 'place' being equally as tangible as a physical location and as intangible as the instinctive feeling of belonging – or not, as the case may be.

Before exploring these examples of topophilia, it would be useful to put the term in some context, both historical and definitional. Yi-Fu Tuan's detailed and ranging *Topophilia: A Study of Environmental Perception, Attitudes and Values* (1974) is the first work to explore the concept in significant depth. Importantly, he considers 'place' as not only a physical location, but also a phenomenon rendered meaningful by human experience[11]. Further to this, the British-American academic John Agnew sets out a three-part conception of

[11] Tuan, Yi-Fu, *Topophilia: A Study of Environmental Perception, Attitudes and Values*.

place, centring on **locale** (a setting for everyday interactions), **location** (the macro effects arising out of the relationship between places) and **sense of place** (personal conceptions derived from lived experience)[12]. Agnew's framing is not dissimilar to that of Doreen Massey, where place is seen 'as articulated moments in networks of social relations and understandings...'[13]. It is this definition – essentially a combination of Agnew's locale and sense of place – which will be pertinent in this book.

The concept of place may also be informed by nomenclature. Designations, for instance, have the potential 'to trigger a series of narratives, subjects and understandings.'[14] In the context of topophilia, this observation could imply a link between the details contained within toponyms and the feelings that a place inspires. 'Understandings' involve cognitive processes, which add substance and meaning to place – or 'sense of place' in Agnew's terms.

Turning to its etymology briefly, Tim Cresswell explains its emergence in Ancient Greece. Plato uses the terms 'chora' (region) and 'topos' (place), where the former is a portion of space set apart from 'keon' (void), whilst the latter 'refers to an achieved place – the product of a process of becoming.' In contrast, Aristotle defines 'chora' as a 'large region of country while "topos" would describe a smaller scale place within it.'[15]

Understandings of topophilia do not finish here. Relph points out that it has become adopted in musical and artistic senses, as well as

---

[12] Agnew, John, *Place and Politics*, pp5-6.
[13] Massey, Doreen, 'A Global Sense of Place', *Marxism Today*, p28.
[14] Agnew, John and Corbridge, Stuart, *Mastering Space*, p48.
[15] Cresswell, Tim, *Place: An Introduction*, p25.

continuing to extend itself in academic quarters[16]. It is even, if gradually, reaching into UK secondary education, by means of the AQA A Level Geography syllabus[17].

Importantly, comprehending topophilia entails some acquaintance with the contrasting concept, topophobia, also apparent in Holmes' script. Topophobia, or 'fear of place' is outlined by Relph in terms of those spaces which trigger a 'persistent rejection', such as 'the landscapes of the coal mining areas of Appalachia.'[18] Topophobia might also be associated with very specific feelings of dread, such as a fear of crime or the loss of a friend catalysing bleak associations for a place[19]. This place-based phobia is considered on highly personal grounds in Dylan Trigg's *Topophobia: A Phenomenology of Anxiety* (2016). Here, the author considers the associations between place and states of emotional distress.

Turning to where love of place and fear of place occur in 'The Mysterious Planet', it will be useful to consider three contrasting pairings, each of which presents both topophilic and topophobic experiences.

---

[16] Relph, 'Topophilia and Topophils'.

[17] Bowen, Ann, et al, *Geography Student Book*.

[18] Relph, 'The Phenomenological Foundations of Geography', Department of Geography, University of Toronto. Discussion Paper No 21, p28.

[19] Šimáček, Petr, Šerý, Milosav, Fiedor, David and Brisudová, Lucia, 'To Fear or Not to Fear? Exploring the Temporality of Topophobia in Urban Environments', *Moravian Geographical Reports*, 28(4); Tuan, Yi-Fu, *Space and Place: The Perspective of Experience*, p140.

Underground, Overground

Holmes presents two, ostensibly diverse, groups; separated yet connected, each evidencing comprehensions of place which present 'persistent appeal' and 'persistent rejection'[20]. On the one hand, there are the Underground Dwellers: 500 souls living in a sterile, sealed-off space, where water rationing is brutally enforced at the behest of an unseen tyrant. On the other, there is the Tribe of the Free: a modestly populated agrarian community, where execution by burning is practised according to the will of a prophesying queen.

For the Underground Dwellers, place is polarised. There explicitly exists that which is below and that which is above. The former represents alleged security, but at the considerable price of freedom and the ever-present threat of the cullings. The latter represents a fearful terra incognita, whose identity rests in a handful of bygone texts and a vague knowledge of a world-devastating fireball. Whatever its true origins, Drathro's workers see this fiery visitant as a natural disaster, shaping their phobia of the surface environment. Landscape architect and academic Jacky Bowring explains how such events, like earthquakes, can cause people to reframe their perceptions of landscape from one of safety to 'scepticism and even fear.'[21] In this case, topophobia is a powerful means of control. Living in a constant state of anxiety, the Underground Dwellers are convinced that their hermetically contained habitat is their only survival option. That they are kept ignorant of the true nature of the

---

[20] Relph, 'The Phenomenological Foundations of Geography', p28.
[21] Bowring, Jacky, 'Topophilia and Topophobia in the Post-Earthquake Landscape of Christchurch, New Zealand', *Revista Geográfica del Sur* 4(6), p109.

surface shows how topophobic conditions may be engineered. The same topophobic force gives purchase to the cullings: the dreaded population control, presumably established due to the restricted resources of their physical enclosure.

If topophobia is central to this underland community, then what room is there for topophilia? We suggest that love of place might yet reside in its places of learning. This is where the figure of Balazar may offer us some direction. His modest character arc is a positive one, redemptive even, as he transitions from naïve scholar, embedded in a binary world where the protective conditions of Marb Station are set against an apparently terrible overground, to burgeoning pioneer of a new society. Hence, this personal journey figures in terms of reconciliation of place, the surface becoming no longer a reason for topophobic feelings, but rather a space to be experienced emotionally – Agnew's sense of place.

The possibility of this transformation arguably lies in Balazar's role as 'reader of the books.'[22] This duty centres on guardianship of Marb Station's three sacred tomes, which not only reference the world before the fireball, but also describe some of its habitats, both factual and fictive. This slim collection points to a repositioning of place as something imaginable, comprehensible qualities which may allow Balazar to entertain topophilic leanings and so move away from the anxieties aroused by the surface.

The leader of the train guard, Merdeen, may also tend towards feelings of topophilia. He is perfectly aware of the true nature of the

---

[22] 'The Mysterious Planet' Part One. All dialogue quoted from 'The Mysterious Planet' unless stated otherwise.

surface and presumably has observed it firsthand. Caught within the power of Drathro, Merdeen uses his position to smuggle Underground Dwellers to the surface, where they can join the Tribe of the Free. As such, it would be reasonable for him to associate positive feelings with the world above, which represents escape from the Immortal's oppressive regime. As Merdeen pointedly observes, 'I am sick of the cullings.'[23]

Insomuch as the surface may offer elements of topophilia to Balazar and Merdeen, it contains a mix of sentiments for the members of the Tribe of the Free. Queen Katryca, who seeks wisdom in fiery divination, exercises near-absolute authority in this preindustrial society. Yet her capacity to project her power is limited. Bereft of the weapons carried by 'star travellers', insecurity and fear would not be unsurprising responses, even in such a monarch. In contrast is her trusted lieutenant, Broken Tooth. As a former Underground Dweller, Broken Tooth must have felt topophobic sensations about the surface. His transition to life in the open air would very likely have been dramatic. It is possible, then, that he experienced some degree of psychological discombobulation, what Trigg calls 'spatiotemporal homesickness'[24]. Managing this change would mean adjusting to an entirely novel life context; phenomenologically speaking, a new 'life-world'[25]. On the topophilic side of things, Broken Tooth has naturalistic skills, such as tracking, which reveal not only a practical

---

[23] Part Two.

[24] Trigg, Dylan, *Topophobia: A Phenomenology of Anxiety*, pxxi.

[25] Relph, 'The Phenomenological Foundations of Geography', p3. A 'lifeworld' is an individual's complete, direct and subjective lived experience, as developed in the phenomenological philosophy of Edmund Husserl.

awareness of the outward world, but also a deeply experiential connection with it. This psychological linkage represents a sizable factor in love of place, further demonstrated in his loyalty to his adopted home. Such a feeling is seen in those who become inextricably bonded to their surroundings. This is noted by the nature writer Roger Morgan-Grenville. His visit to Scotland's Sandwood Bay, and the work there of the John Muir Trust, sees him remarking of one of the volunteers that, 'He is imbued with the deepest sense of place that only somewhere with the rawness of these peat flows and dark pools can bestow… he has married into it both physically and metaphorically.'[26]

In these two communities, then, topophilia is framed in notions of safety (Underground Dwellers) and freedom (Tribe of the Free), an 'urban-rural continuum' existing between them[27]. In contrast, topophobia lies in a spatial dichotomy: the interconnected, pre-fireball world – what Massey calls 'time-space-compression'[28] – erased and in its place two disparate groups, neither of which possesses a genuine picture of the other, their mutual ignorance helping to inspire fear of place.

Looking at love of place and fear of place from the perspective of these small-scale communities involves a wide-angle lens, with topophilic and topophobic attitudes presented in largely macroscopic terms. To diverge from this approach, we must consider

---

[26] Morgan-Grenville, Roger, *Across A Waking Land*, p278.

[27] Bowen et al, *Geography Student Book*, p320.

[28] Massey, 'A Global Sense of Place', p24. The phenomenon 'time-space compression' refers to the world seeming smaller due to improvements in transport infrastructure.

these emotional states on an individual basis.

Awe, Sorrow

Twirling his umbrella to demonstrate how much Ravolox and Earth are alike, the Doctor presents Peri with a mystery that, in the Time Lord's words, is nothing short of a 'phenomenon'. Peri's more poetic reply, that her surroundings recall to her 'a wet November back on Earth,'[29] cuts to the heart of the matter. Nearing the entrance to some sort of underground space, she comments on a feeling of déjà vu. It is not a pleasant sensation, and it encourages her to try and quit the otherwise peaceful woodland scene. This growing intuition on Peri's part, in finding familiarity in what is ostensibly an alien world, foreshadows the imminent revelation that Ravolox **is** Earth. Later, when she uncovers a Marble Arch Underground station sign, and the Doctor attempts to apply some scepticism to her discovery, Peri's retort is as emotive as it is instinctive: 'I know it is. I can feel it.'[30]

Peri's reaction is also one of sorrow. Amongst the darkened ruins of a once bustling corner of the City of Westminster, she makes a powerful point about the planet as a whole: 'This cinder we're standing on is all that's left of my world.'[31] Her remark is understandable, which hints at more than a purely emotional outburst. There is a profound dislocation here, despite two light years and millions of years between her late 20th-century Earth and the time of Ravolox. This is because she is confronting a collision of

---

[29] Part One.
[30] Part One.
[31] Part One.

feelings, from her dismissal of Ravolox in her opening comment –'I don't think I like Ravolox very much'[32] – to her comprehending that this unremarkable spot, recovered from an apparent solar devastation, is actually her home planet. The brute fact of her distress points to a qualitative phenomenon, revealing the efficacy of place to bring about considerable mental states.

There is an empirical point here, too. When Peri exclaims that Ravolox is all that remains of 'Everything I knew'[33] she is asserting a key psychological point. All that she understood of herself is contained in a celestial body which, in her estimation, amounts to an altogether different place. Yet, at the same time, it **is** one and the same place. This is where topophilia, in the form of her attachment to Earth, and topophobia, in the form of her distress at the real identity of Ravolox, collide in a kind of psychological nausea. At best, this experience is disorientating; at worst, it is highly distressing. It is no surprise, then, that when she is offered the chance to explore the world concealed beneath the ruins of the Marble Arch Underground station, she declines, preferring to wait at its former entrance, where 'they used to sell candy bars and newspapers'[34]. Shades of topophobia, perhaps, or a sort of topo-melancholia, arising from deep within her psyche.

Although Peri's upset is not assuaged by the Doctor's eulogising on the immensity of time, he does empathise with her – 'I know how you feel'[35] – and seeks to comfort her by pointing out that her Earth,

---

[32] Part One.
[33] Part One.
[34] Part One.
[35] Part One.

temporally speaking, is secure. In this sequence of emotional triage, the Doctor signals his awareness of place in and of itself as something which can resonate powerfully with those who encounter it. There is something else in the Doctor's actions, however, which points to his place awareness as something rare and nuanced. He is equally comfortable, for instance, managing the confusions of Balazar as he is trying to convince Queen Katryca of his sincerity, never mind his efforts to persuade an impossibly stubborn Drathro. This confidence of place in a social context – Agnew's second strand – may point to his feeling at home almost anywhere, his countless years of space-time travel informing this special quality. Moreover, when he talks to Peri about 'the exhilarating smell of a freshly laundered forest,'[36] and only a short while later hints at the epic life cycles of planets and stars, it is clear that his perception of place has the most extraordinary flexibility, shifting from close view to telescopic with equal fluency. It is this unique perspective on place (which we might call the 'deep-field' view) that may best summarise the sense of place of a traveller in the fourth dimension.

For the Doctor and Peri, place is perceived in diverging ways: one informed by an earthly/temporal mindset, the other understood in extra-terrestrial/atemporal terms. Of the pair, there is some onus on the Doctor to reach out to Peri, which he does; he offers her his support as she seeks to process her cognisance of Ravolox's identity. After all, he too must have undergone similar experiences on first leaving Gallifrey, however much his comparatively longer lifespan may have softened the shock by this point.

---

[36] Part One.

In the last of our pairings, such a contrast is sharpened still further, as human framings of place, whether good or ill, are set against the unyielding logic of machine intelligence.

Logos, Pathos

Within the subterranean world of the Underground Dwellers, and set apart in its own private chamber, is Drathro, the L3 robot. Known simply as 'the Immortal' by the humans at its command, Drathro exists within a rigidly rational picturing of reality, the limits of which demand the use of gifted humans to offer a way out of its slavish ratiocination.

Drathro's backstory is intriguing. The robot exists to protect the Sleepers from Andromeda, a mysterious group, unseen in this adventure, who have stolen Time Lord secrets and stored them on Earth[37]. With the arrival of the fireball (read Gallifreyan magnetron), Drathro establishes a survival chamber for the Sleepers, with the capacity to sustain several hundred human survivors. This population becomes the Underground Dwellers, complete with a mini-library and security detail, known as the train guard. Place, for Drathro, is orderly and controlled, a veritable buttress, in fact, against the inevitable march of entropy. Ironically, it is the Second Law of Thermodynamics which is the author of Drathro's most serious challenge: a failing power source[38]. This is where the tradition of recruiting the two most capable youths from each generation of

---

[37] As confirmed in 'The Ultimate Foe' episode 1 (*The Trial of a Time Lord* Part Thirteen).

[38] The second of four principles which govern energy transfer and transformation, the Second Law of Thermodynamics states that in a closed system disorder (entropy) always increases.

Underground Dwellers comes into play (a conceit which Holmes deployed in his first **Doctor Who** script, *The Krotons*). These young tyros are tasked with solving Drathro's energy problem; the assumption being that their ability to take intuitive shortcuts will speed up the work. By the time of the Doctor's arrival, the youths concerned are Humker and Tandrell, whose plain white garb lends them the appearance of lab technicians.

Drathro's sense of place appears to be a purely rational construction, ringfenced by the prescriptions of reason. As such, however much Drathro has the capacity to learn, its 'processors of ratiocination are logical.'[39] Hemmed in by a mode of thought that cannot recognise, never mind entertain, intuitive thinking, Drathro is forced to follow a painfully slow heuristic model, utterly devoid of imaginative process. Yet, when the Doctor engages in one last attempt to shut down Drathro's power system, the robot resists his interference and flatly states 'All that you see is my creation.' Paradoxically, then, Drathro's regard for place may be predicated on a sense of creative ownership, even a feeling of hubris, as the Doctor later observes. Thus, place is not just the physical or psychological space represented by the domain of the Underground Dwellers, it is also evidence of a god-like creator, who perceives the inhabitants of their survival chamber as existing 'only to serve'.

So, do topophilia or topophobia hold any meaning for Drathro? As a machine that acts according to the protocols contained in its software, it seems improbable that it could experience the sort of mental states aroused by these phenomena. But there is an arrogance in how it perceives the Underground Dwellers, possibly an

---

[39] Part Two.

egotism too, which departs from what we might expect of a purely rational mechanism. Centuries as the 'Immortal' in its 'castle' may have distorted Drathro's self-proclaimed logical ratiocination, allowing just the merest hint of irrationality to enter into its mental workings, to say nothing of entropy steadily breaking down its systems. Given this, where might topophilic or topophobic sentiments seep into this machine's conceptual scheme? Drathro's private chamber – its so-called castle – represents a safe space, where it can methodically enact its plan, insulated from the variables arising from the human community inhabiting its wider living space. Topophilia might, therefore, exist in this restricted area, where Drathro can choose to operate in an entirely self-contained way. Conversely, the world above, with its potential for the uncontrollable, might be a trigger for negative, even topophobic, reactions in Drathro's reasoning. This, perhaps, is why, when its black light energy source threatens a devastating explosion, it is utterly disinterested in safeguarding the human lives for which it has been responsible for half a millennium. In brutal fashion, Drathro states, 'If I am doomed, then you are all doomed.'[40] For the guardian of the Sleepers from Andromeda, it seems topophilia lies in order, topophobia in disorder.

Drathro's human assistants, Humker and Tandrell, stand in direct contrast to their robotic overlord. Tasked with resolving the problem of its failing power source, these pallid pupils of logic glory in dexterity of thought, proffering syllogistic reasoning and verbal precision with machine-like efficiency. Beyond their rationality, however, these human calculators are a very different proposition,

---

[40] Part Four.

one whose logicality is paper thin. The extent of their emotional register first surfaces when they begin to plot their escape from their master's lair. The Doctor's blunt warnings of imminent disaster and the breaching of the underground shelter by Queen Katryca and her warriors, force desperate measures on Drathro's algorithmic apprentices. It is, however, a desperation which sees a frantic crash of feelings, topophilic and topophobic. In Drathro's chamber they are safe, albeit trapped in a narrow, isolated environ. Planted in this hi-tech world as callow youths, now they must transition again, only this time there is not a moment to acclimatise, no space to manage the translocation they must undergo if they are to survive. Whatever topophobic sentiment they might hold about the surface quickly evaporates as they leave behind their sealed-off world and breathe in unfiltered air for the very first time. Tandrell quickly exclaims 'What a wonderful smell.' only for Humker to concur that 'you're right. Absolutely wonderful.'[41] A love of place conditioned in a flash-freeze moment of olfactory delight.

Humker and Tandrell are human beings, whose emotions have been concealed beneath an accretion of logic. In opposition, Drathro is a machine, whose cast-iron rationality has become rusted to the point of vanity. Whereas Humker and Tandrell are offered a new life in a single breath of air, Drathro is doomed by its own foolish survivalism. Here, then, are two distinct understandings of place: one human, yet caught in the inflexible mountings of machine logic; the other robotic, yet contained within the flaws of a human-like arrogance.

---

[41] Part Four.

CHAPTER 2: RAVOLOX, PLACE AND DWELLING

Attachment to place is a complex phenomenon. It entails an intricate net of psycho-physical conditions[42]. It involves human experience and social framings[43]. It is increasingly understood in a range of terms, and can be appreciated in both positive and negative ways[44]. Naturally, attachment to urban places may differ from that to rural places, the latter being a potential trigger for topophobic feelings[45]. Exploring this event in its totality, with its deeply interwoven quantitative and qualitative features, would prove overwhelming. However, adopting a somewhat philosophical, if not existential, approach may offer a direction that is more accessible.

The German thinker Martin Heidegger argues that only human beings have the capacity to encounter their surroundings in both theoretical and practical ways. By this, he means not only our perception of objects and spaces, but also our capacity to experience concern for them. This unique understanding is a key part of human existence. If a human being can interact with the world in this way, then they exist in a situation which Heidegger calls 'dwelling' in the world[46]. This is a subtle condition, however, which may be 'harassed by work, made insecure by the hunt for gain and success, bewitched by the entertainment and recreation industry.'[47] Nevertheless,

---

[42] Tuan, *Space and Place*, p141.
[43] Tuan, *Topophilia*, passim; Massey, 'A Global Sense of Place', p28.
[44] Relph, 'Topophilia and Topophils'; Tuan, *Topophilia*; Relph, 'The Phenomenological Foundations of Geography', p.28.
[45] Thurgill, James, 'A Fear of the Folk: On Topophobia and the Horror of Rural Landscapes'.
[46] Mulhall, Stephen, *Heidegger and Being and Time*, pp41-44.
[47] Heidegger, Martin , *Poetry, Language, Thought*, p211.

Heidegger is adamant that our human nature 'means to dwell,' since 'we are **dwellers.**'[48] Although this thought-scape is extensive, elements of it may bear upon the ideas in this chapter. As such, Heidegger's notion of ontological concern, and its realisation through the act of dwelling, may be found in the ways and means by which some characters in 'The Mysterious Planet' interact with their respective environments, thus revealing Ravolox to be not only a future Earth but also an unusually sophisticated geo-philosophical locus[49].

Naturally, the complexity of location is determined by the complexity of perception. But properly understanding perception is a difficult business. Scrutinising its workings is predicated on traditional sciences, such as anthropology, psychology and biology, which, according to Heidegger, may not offer a complete answer to the human condition[50]. To try and frame this project in less orthodox terms, then, we will use a sampling of place-related literature, which employs not only geographical and historical vectors, but also those of a social, artistic and philosophical nature. These include Nan Shepherd's intimate description of Scotland's Cairngorm mountains in *The Living Mountain* (1977), Roger Scruton's thoughts on late 20th-century British rural life in *News from Somewhere* (2004), JA Baker's meticulous observations of peregrine falcons in the Essex marshlands in *The Peregrine* (1967), and a journey through Britain's

---

[48] Heidegger, *Poetry, Language, Thought*, pp145-46 (author's emphasis).
[49] The term 'ontological' refers to matters of being and existence and entails questions such as 'What is real?'.
[50] Heidegger, Martin, *Being and Time*, pp74-75.

waterways in Roger Deakin's *Waterlog* (1996). We will also draw on the ideas of Cambridge scholar Robert Macfarlane and author Nick Hunt, both of whom have written extensively on understandings of place and landscape, through the medium of walking.

In addition, this chapter uses a further layer of navigation by dividing according to the four elements of Ancient Greek cosmology. The first section considers the element of fire, which lies at the heart of the Underground Dwellers' identity; Shepherd's mountainscapes, forged in the cauldron of tectonic physics are considered here. The second part, framed through the element of earth, examines the relationship between the Tribe of the Free and the surface of Ravolox, where Scruton's insightful examination of soil bears relevance. The Tribe of the Free also acts as the focus of the next element, air, with their totemic worship hinting at Baker's sky-gazing peregrinations. Finally, the element of water defines the survival of the Underground Dwellers, given anchorage by Deakin's memoir of wild swimming.

But let us begin with a planet-wrecking event and a group of human survivors, whose sense of place and historical consciousness are fundamentally shaped by this awesome happening.

Fire

Fire is a powerful phenomenon. Cosmologically, it is at the beginning of our universe, where an inconceivably superheated explosion gave rise to time and space. Mythologically, it is a priceless commodity, wrested from the slopes of a jealous Mount Olympus by Prometheus and presented as the catalyst to human progress (a literal starting point for **Doctor Who**, too, in 'The Cave of Skulls' (*An Unearthly Child* (1963) episode 2)). Fire is also central in the history of Ravolox.

Whether seen as a natural event or the result of Time Lord technology, the conflagration which devastates the planet is both a cultural artefact and a temporal marker. In the case of the former, it gives the inhabitants of Marb Station a reason for their subterranean confinement. Not unlike the Starliner's procedure-trapped passengers in Andrew Smith's *Full Circle* (1980), the figures of Merdeen and Balazar, along with every other Underground Dweller, inhabit a determined space, where a centuries-old catastrophe dictates the conditions of the present – at least as it is interpreted by Drathro's inflexible thinking. In the case of the latter, the fireball is both a year zero and a tabula rasa, whereby that which came before it is completely set apart, as though belonging to an altogether different reality[51].

Fire, then, is critical to the history of the Underground Dwellers, and the author of their Drathro-driven economy, which produces a diet of gruel-like food, washed down by rationed water. Yet, just as the titular Greek king in Albert Camus' *The Myth of Sisyphus* (1942) is condemned endlessly to roll a boulder up a mountain, but experiences freedom whilst descending the mountain, the Underground Dwellers may also embrace a kind of liberty within their bounded setting; a liberty constituted by how they encounter the limited space around them, whether actual or metaphorical, therefore touching upon not only Agnew's sense of place but also Relph's 'life-world' with its intricate arrangement of 'ambiguities,

---

[51] A 'tabula rasa' is literally a 'blank table', though usually translated from Latin as 'blank slate', meaning an opportunity to start from scratch.

commitments and meanings in which we are inextricably involved'[52].

To find such complication amongst the geometric architecture of their world, the Underground Dwellers may turn to their humble library. This unusual collection, with its government work on migratory wildfowl, a Victorian fairy tale and a 19th-century US classic, presents an account of life before the fire which, although incredibly slender in its scope, still raises important questions on ethics and the environment. Balazar, the wistful Reader of the Books, is clearly drawn to these queries. When remarking to the Doctor, for example, on Marb Station's 'Books of Knowledge' he observes that they 'contain much wisdom for those who can interpret their meaning.'[53] His tone, if nothing else, implies that he thinks such interpretations are not beyond his reach. Capable or not, Balazar's engagement with these pre-fireball depictions points to an understanding of place which reaches beyond traditional descriptive or explanatory devices.

Such a mindset may be found in Nan Shepherd's *The Living Mountain*. This extraordinary piece of writing, which Robert Macfarlane defines as 'one of the two most remarkable 20th-century British studies of landscape that I know', sees Shepherd gradually experience Scotland's Cairngorms – a place with which she was intimately acquainted throughout her life – unfiltered by the usual biases, perceptual or otherwise, which we carry with us[54]. She comments that, with age, she 'began to discover the mountain in

---

[52] Agnew, *Place and Politics*, pp5-6; Relph, 'The Phenomenological Foundations of Geography', p3.
[53] Part One.
[54] Shepherd, Nan, *The Living Mountain*, pxiii.

itself,' and that 'The thing to be known grows with the knowing.' Shepherd goes so far as to frame this process in Buddhist terms, whereby the act of going into the life of the mountain is just as much about going into one's own life, thus it is no less than 'a journey into Being'[55].

In her wonderings, Shepherd describes a life-world which can be mapped and remapped, unpicked and unpacked, until we are able to engage with it on its own terms, perhaps all the while approaching Heidegger's conception of dwelling. Balazar's time as Reader of the Books may afford him this possibility. By meditating on his tomes, assisted by their modest number, he may begin to develop an awareness, if not a comprehension, of Ravoloxian place as defined by the solar phenomenon which forged it. In this way, Prometheus' gift is not just a catalyst for exponential growth, but also a stimulant for topographical meaning.

If the fireball, whether through historical placement or cultural significance, can stimulate reflective thinking on the nature of place – not dissimilar to Shepherd's experiences in the Cairngorms – then the surface of Ravolox, as experienced by the Tribe of the Free, may act as its complement, one which is given shape and form by the earth itself.

Earth

The contrast between the Tribe of the Free and the Underground Dwellers could not be less unambiguous. Whilst Drathro's work units are yoked to the L3's interminable procedures, Queen Katryca's people live under open sky in a quasi-medieval society, where

[55] Shepherd, *The Living Mountain*, p108.

divination dictates justice and survival is rooted in the land. There are no Books of Knowledge to consult, only their leader's flame-fed prophesying. Their experience of Ravolox as a life-world is an empirical one, light years away from the rational reflections of Balazar and his fellows. In this way, the Tribe of the Free offers an alternative awareness of place, and perhaps dwelling, which may help to complete a 'place picture', if you will, of Ravolox.

The earthy and largely untamed portion of Ravolox in which they live is both the subject of their place awareness and the space in which their experience of place arises. Limited to raising crops and livestock by pre-industrial means, their relationship with the natural world is one entirely unknown to the Underground Dwellers. Whereas Balazar must imagine the migration cycle of the Canada goose as best he can, for the Tribe of the Free it may be possible to spy skeins of such birds as they fly to and from their feeding grounds. It is this proximity to the land and the species it supports that gives Broken Tooth and his compatriots such a singular perspective on their world. This is explored by the philosopher Roger Scruton, who writes on the power of the land in the lives of the people who work it. To plough the soil, observes Scruton, is to perform an act of settling, by which we 'become one with it'[56]. He goes on to argue that each of us has an integral attachment to the soil, perhaps touching upon Shepherd's 'journey into Being'[57]. On Ravolox, this conjoining of humanity and earth is manifested in the Tribe of the Free and perhaps in the meditations of Balazar, too. But, for the Tribe, it is an understanding of place which entails an unforgiving context. As Scruton points out,

---

[56] Scruton, Roger, *News from Somewhere*, p2.
[57] Shepherd, *The Living Mountain*, p108.

the 'curmudgeonly soil' of the claylands in which he lives 'turns health into sickness, youth into old age; and life, in due course, into death.' It may also influence temperament[58]. It is no wonder, then, that Katryca operates in absolutes, whether in choosing to execute Glitz at the behest of a flaming vision, or to confront the age-old Immortal head on. Still, this rough life also admits of a cognisance of place which is immediate and profound – two qualities which may be absent from the lives of the Underground Dwellers in their sealed-off world.

The land on which the Tribe of the Free subsists is only part of their picturing of place. If we accept the Doctor's remark that around half a millennium has passed since the solar fireball swept across Ravolox and forced its human survivors to quit the surface, then the extent of any natural regeneration (irrespective of whether the fire was as devastating as Time Lord records would have it) would be considerable. In such a place, any remnant of infrastructure, never mind complete buildings, would soon vanish under a mantle of grass and woody undergrowth. A similar situation is apparent in the surroundings of the former nuclear plant at Chernobyl. Here, in the years since the 1986 disaster, research has found that 'the net environmental effect of the accident has been much greater biodiversity and abundance of species,' to the extent that the exclusion zone around the facility has 'become a unique sanctuary for wildlife due to the absence of humans.'[59] A world untrodden, never mind unfarmed, for so many centuries may be likewise, thus giving the Tribe of the Free an understanding of place and dwelling

---

[58] Scruton, *News from Somewhere*, pp4-5.

[59] World Nuclear Association, 'Chernobyl Accident 1986'.

hewn from the effort of reclaiming it.

Unchecked nature, devoid of human settlement, can be forbidding. These areas may instil feelings of topophobia[60]. Where nature and its inhabitants are anthropomorphised, the same holds true. Richard Adams' *Watership Down* (1972) tells how some animals give a wide berth to 'close woodland, where the ground is shady, damp and grassless',[61] whilst Kenneth Grahame's Mole sees the Wild Wood of Badger as 'low and threatening, like a black reef in some still southern sea.'[62] Human beings, too, have long seen forestlands as distinct from the tilled fields of the farm. Britain's recent history of clearance emphasises this perception. In the 20th century alone, over half of its ancient woodland was felled and replaced with regimented ranks of pine forest[63]. Thus, its status as a 'dominion of trees' was undone by civilisation emerging out of the forestscape, the tree-line demarcating the compass of human progress[64]. For the Tribe of the Free, this difference gives traction to their experience of place. They too are charged with building a home amidst ancient woodlands, thus reenacting the original encounter between settled humanity and the world of wood, water and stone.

This sense of place, expressed in Scruton's conception of settling, is mirrored by the totem worship of Katryca's people. Set firmly within the soil, this practice also looks skywards, towards an entirely different location, where landscape becomes cloudscape and the

---

[60] Gaspar de Freitas, Joana, 'Landscapes of Fear: The Portuguese Coast', p29.
[61] Adams, Richard, *Watership Down*, p34.
[62] Grahame, Kenneth, *The Wind in the Willows*, p36.
[63] Macfarlane, Robert, *The Wild Places*, p9.
[64] Macfarlane, *The Wild Places*, pp91-92.

ordinary perceptions of depth and distance are rendered meaningless.

Air

Whilst the Underground Dwellers have a restricted understanding of the underland in which their survival chamber is submerged, their grasp of Ravolox's atmosphere – Heidegger's 'vaulting path of the sun' – is non-existent[65]. Balazar's cogitating on the Canada goose, for instance, necessitates a true leap of the imagination, as he tries to conjure up an environment utterly alien to anything he has encountered. Conversely, for the Tribe of the Free, this part of Ravolox's ecology meets them throughout their lives; it frames the seasons, sets the weather and gives up that most vital resource, water. Also, it offers guidance on near-future conditions. For a community whose survival depends not just on farming but also on foraging and hunting, this is a crucial point. To be so attuned to this space, however, requires an instinct that draws on the portents of the sky. Such awareness must be based on an especial accumulation of experiences – a point recognised by Tuan, who observes that it is human experience which 'commands his subject matter and themes'[66].

Such experiential sky-scaping has shades of Gerard Manley Hopkins' 'inscape', which denotes the unique quality of something[67]. Shepherd's deep-field gazing is here, too. As Macfarlane points out

---

[65] Heidegger, *Poetry, Language, Thought*, p147.
[66] Tuan, *Space and Place*, pv.
[67] Hopkins, Gerard Manley, *Look Up at the Skies! Poems and Prose*, p10.

in his introduction to *The Living Mountain*, she 'came to know the Cairngorms 'deeply' rather than 'widely'[68]. This sort of fine-print perception works to comprehend a single space through direct experience over an expanded period of time. JA Baker's tracking of peregrine falcons across the marshes and estuary lands of his native Essex echoes this mindset. It transforms vision, for instance, as the 'land flows out from the eye in deltas of piercing colour,' and dictates the passage of time[69]. And it draws on horizons, which 'layer the memory like strata.'[70]. In his short essay 'On the Essex Coast', Baker is also adamant on the magnitude of the firmament, of which he bluntly observes that man is a 'cringing figure under the vast power and solitude of the sky.'[71].

Baker's reference to solitude is striking. It is the isolation of the hunter – the peregrine falcon diving at its quarry in 'hundred-foot vertical jabs.'[72] Broken Tooth, another sort of hunter, traces the escaped star travellers through signs on the ground, a language of the earth. Yet he surely needs an understanding of the dynamic space above ground too. Where birds are put to flight by a disturbance, for instance, their hurried trajectories may give notice of a prey's presence; a scent caught on the wind might hint at carrion not far off and the corresponding chance of catching its author; and the curvature of a cloud may foreshadow an approaching tempest and the need to find shelter. Thus, this fragile film of gases which encircles Ravolox provides signs and tokens to those with the skills

---

[68] Shepherd, *The Living Mountain*, pxv.
[69] Baker, JA, *The Peregrine*, p31.
[70] Baker, *The Peregrine*, p27.
[71] Baker, *The Peregrine*, p214.
[72] Baker, *The Peregrine*, p71.

to interpret them (even forecasting imminent earthquakes, according to the former chemist, Zhonghao Shou[73]). Place, therefore, becomes an admixture of barely conscious conceptions, harvested from sense data moving as fast as the strongest winds.

The long-distance walker and writer Nick Hunt considers the cultural and historical purchase of this force in exploring four of Europe's strongest winds. Reflecting on his experience of the powerful Bora, a gale-force easterly which tears across the Balkans and the north-east flanks of Italy, he observes that 'it was less a sound than a sensation, a nameless energetic **thing** that erased the line between hearing and feeling.'[74] Hunt's description of his stormy encounter, high above Croatia's coastal city of Split, reveals how sensory understandings are confounded by elemental forces – but still need to be unpacked and processed, largely at a subconscious level, to create the sort of fundamental grasp of place which Shepherd and Baker, inter alia, possess in spades.

Only a short way from this story of sky and place lies a hermetically-sealed survivalist society, where water is so precious that its theft is punished by summary stoning. Within this hyper-controlled space, understandings of place and feelings of dwelling take on an existential urgency.

Water

Within moments of entering Marb Station, the Doctor discovers the value of water for Drathro's work units. Examining a flask of liquid, he inadvertently sets off an alarm, a computerised voice declaring

---

[73] Pretor-Pinney, Gavin, *The Cloudspotter's Guide*, pp189-93.
[74] Hunt, Nick, *Where the Wild Winds Are*, p123 (author's emphasis).

'Water thief. Water thief. Protect your water.'[75] In seconds, the Doctor is rushed by a group of Underground Dwellers and clubbed to the ground. Regaining consciousness, the Time Lord learns that water is so rare in this electric-lit world that those who threaten it face the ultimate sanction, its scarcity informing the psychologies of Balazar and his peers, sharpening their conception of dwelling in the bleakest of terms.

For the Underground Dwellers, water is a priceless commodity. The notion of using it for anything other than daily survival would be unthinkable. Water as transport? Absurd. Water as recreation? Still more absurd. But on a planet where this substance is in abundance, these notions should be commonplace. Wild swimmer and environmentalist Roger Deakin details the wider significance of water as a perspective on place, amongst other things, in his work *Waterlog*. Variously an advertising copywriter, teacher and documentary maker, Deakin was inspired by John Cheever's short story 'The Swimmer' to embark on a year-long wild swimming odyssey through Britain. He imagines that in 'following water, flowing with it...' he will get 'under the skin of things, of learning something new.' Along the way, he finds childhood memories reawakened, histories explored, and, perhaps above all else, the British landscape rewired in aquatic terms; his 'frog's-eye view' allowing him to see something as routine as rainfall in a quite different way, the sky mirrored in the water 'full of tiny dancers: water sprites springing up on tiptoe like bright pins over the surface.'[76] Compared with Peri's dismissive take on a rainy Ravolox,

---

[75] Part One.

[76] Deakin, Roger, *Waterlog*, pp1-3.

Deakin's aesthetic picturing of precipitation is a watercolour delight; a variance surely derived from a very different conception of place, where water is an all-enveloping phenomenon, far removed from Drathro's draconian restrictions.

Peri's pithy pronouncement on Ravolox's terrestrial character echoes an equally laconic observation by Edwardian diarist Edith Holden. In an entry from autumn 1906, Holden writes of a 'Steady drizzle of rain, – a regular November day.'[77] Her economic turn of phrase is not typical of her writings. Holden's poetry sampling, folklore references and finely-sketched illustrations, combine with gentle remarks on the turn of the seasons to present a style of journaling which encourages a meditative mindset – not unlike Deakin's 'frog's-eye view'. Deakin's wild swimming is anchored by his own private pool, bordering his Suffolk farmhouse; a moat in fact, most likely dating back to the 1500s, which 'is constantly renewing and repainting itself.'[78] For Balazar, such an idea, never mind its liquid reality, resides exclusively within the pages of a book. Three books, to be precise. Marb Station's Books of Knowledge all describe places where water is abundant: the habitat of the Canada goose; an ocean-going white whale; and a Victorian yarn where a boy chimney sweep falls into a river and is transformed into a water-baby. These watery backdrops present ironic juxtapositions with Balazar's own water-starved existence. In this way, his grasp of place must be affected by imagining a world soaked in H_2O, whilst his own circumstances are, for all intents and purposes, a desert of metal and plastic.

If there is irony in Balazar studying a world where water is a common

---

[77] Holden, Edith, *The Country Diary of an Edwardian Lady*, p155.
[78] Deakin, *Waterlog*, p69.

feature whilst living with a desperate shortage of it, then it is equally ironic that Ravolox's water cycle, as the Doctor and Peri realise, is demonstrably active. Drathro, too, is well aware that 'precipitation has returned to normal', but the robot's machine logic stops it from letting its human population take advantage of this change[79]. Here, perhaps, is where water, in the context of Ravolox, becomes the key agency in understanding place and Heidegger's notion of dwelling. For it is water that inhabits the air as gas, descends upon the land as liquid, percolating and eroding as it goes, thus binding sky to earth. Water also bonds itself to fire, as its counterpart, resisting that most awesome of solar events by ultimately quenching its power, and allowing the earth and the air to recover, as it cycles through its states of being, to restore Ravolox to something like its former terrestrial condition. In the words of a later iteration of the Doctor, 'Water just waits. It wears down the clifftops, the mountains, the whole of the world. Water always wins.'[80]

---

[79] Part Two.

[80] *The Waters of Mars* (2009).

CHAPTER 3: RAVOLOX, LAND AND ECOLOGISM

Dwelling, in a Heideggerian sense, involves an appreciation of place that is existential in its concern[81]. It may also entail ecological leanings[82]. This awareness of, and attachment for, location may arise from several sentiments, including feelings of deep attraction (topophilia), which are not readily explicable but nonetheless are part of ordinary human experience. These locales may also act as oppositional states, which, equally inexplicably, cause a sense of disquiet and even fear[83].

The life of daleswoman Hannah Hauxwell may be a rare example of Heidegger's concept of dwelling in practice. Born in 1926, Hauxwell lived most of her life at Low Birk Hatt, a farm in Baldersdale in the North Pennines. In the early 1970s, her life became the subject of a television documentary. Until then, and for a time thereafter, Hauxwell lived frugally on the produce of her farming, managing without electricity and running water. Yet, despite these privations, her love of her home and the nearby Hunder Beck, whose 'waters sing a song to me', was unwavering. Reflecting on her life in that remote and, in winter at least, unforgiving setting, she once observed that 'I know this place will always be loyal to me [...] It's mine [...] and always will be [...] even when I'm no longer here.'[84] Hauxwell's turn of phrase, described by one critic as

---

[81] Mulhall, *Heidegger and Being and Time*, p41.

[82] Zimmerman, Michael E, 'Rethinking the Heidegger–Deep Ecology Relationship', *Environmental Ethics*, 15(3), pp195-96.

[83] Hamer, Marc, *A Life in Nature: Or How to Catch a Mole*, pp141-42.

[84] Hauxwell, Hannah, and Cockcroft, Barry, *Seasons of My Life: The Story of a Solitary Daleswoman*, p10.

'Wordsworthian', acknowledges a conception of place which goes beyond the purely material and approaches a bond that may be Heideggerian in nature[85].

Hauxwell's life at Low Birk Hatt has unintentional echoes of the 1960s and 1970s UK iteration of the back-to-the-land movement, the mainspring of which, at least in part, was ecological, if not existential. This push for change included literature, such as John Seymour's iconic *The Complete Book of Self-Sufficiency* (1976), television series, such as Terry Nation's **Survivors** (1975-77) and the popular sitcom **The Good Life** (1975-78), and full-fledged communes, such as Laurieston Hall, with its experience of cooperative living[86]. At its heart, this movement embraced ecologically sensitive lifestyles, connecting it to an awareness of place through a form of circularity, whereby feelings of place feed concern for ecology, and concern for ecology drives a deeper appreciation of place – a veritable feedback loop, aligning with a school of thought known as 'ecologism'.

Holmes' Ravoloxian communities may provide us with a pair of valuable, and contrasting, windows on to this circularity. To explore these openings, this section is arranged under four headings. In the first, the issue of resource management vis-à-vis population growth in the context of Drathro's Underground Dwellers is considered, drawing on the ideas of some thinkers in the field, principally Thomas Malthus and Ester Boserup. In the next, the Tribe of the Free act as a backdrop to explore the efforts of those social movements that have sought to reconfigure society to achieve a greater degree of balance

---

[85] Hauxwell and Cockcroft, *Seasons of My Life*, p186.
[86] Upton, Patrick, 'Forty Years Living And Learning', *Reforesting Scotland* (45), p11.

with the natural world, referring to Bolton Hall, Ralph Borsodi and the aforementioned John Seymour. The third section aims to bring these matters into focus through the philosophy and political ideas of ecologism, with an emphasis on the works of Aldo Leopold, EF Schumacher and Arne Næss. In the concluding part, the extent to which, together, the Underground Dwellers and the Tribe of the Free represent a step towards the circular relationship of place and ecology mentioned above is examined. To do this, some of the environmental concerns set out by writers such as George Monbiot are of particular interest, as is a return to the work of Heidegger, and the possible links between his philosophy and broader understandings of nature and place.

A Malthusian Logic

The principle of population growth outstripping natural resources and becoming unsustainable – i.e. exceeding the 'carrying capacity' of a living space – is as old as the hills[87]. Every community, settled or nomadic, isolated or interconnected, is in a constant state of supply and demand; a model of survival made all the more complicated by the rise of global trade. This last point merits emphasising. Eric Beinhocker observes that in a population such as the Yąnomamö, a largely hunter-gatherer people, trade is manifested in possibly thousands of distinct items (e.g. a type of tool or clothing). In the retail business, these items are known as stock keeping units, or SKUs. In comparison, Beinhocker estimates, albeit very approximately, that the industrialised population of New York City

---

[87] Tivy, Joy, and O'Hare, Greg, *Human Impact on the Ecosystem*, p47; Diamond, Jared, *Collapse: How Societies Choose to Fail or Succeed*, p9.

trades in tens of billions of SKUs[88]. The complexity, then, of our resource management cannot be overstated – a point which bears noting as regards the technological world of the Underground Dwellers.

The work of Thomas Malthus offers us an opening here. In his 1798 study *An Essay on the Principle of Population*, Malthus argues that, over time, food production cannot keep pace with population growth, since the latter increases geometrically whilst the former grows arithmetically[89]. He also claims that the only brakes on population growth are war, disease, famine and natural disasters, and that 'moral restraint', by which Malthus means abstinence through delaying marriage or simply not marrying, is the answer[90]. Neo-Malthusians include biologist Paul R Ehrlich, co-author of the 1968 work *The Population Bomb*, and ecologist Garrett Hardin, whose essay of the same year, titled 'The Tragedy of the Commons', explores a thought experiment on the dangers of unregulated resource access, where shared access leads to overuse and the eventual loss of the resource[91].

Others take a more optimistic line by way of school of thought called cornucopianism, which argues that humanity is distinct from and superior to other species, and that the value of non-human species is determined by the degree to which humans can exploit them. Cornucopianism's solution to the population/resource clash is

---

[88] Beinhocker, Eric D, *The Origin of Wealth*, p9.
[89] Malthus, Thomas, *An Essay on the Principle of Population*, pp15-17.
[90] Malthus, *An Essay on the Principle of Population*, p19.
[91] Hardin, Garrett, 'The Tragedy of the Commons'.

increasingly advanced technical fixes[92]. This is the view of the Danish economist Ester Boserup. In the 1960s, Boserup explored land use in a variety of dynamic contexts and, in line with cornucopianism, found that rather than population growth resulting in a decline in prosperity and a rise in poverty, it 'seems to be the cause of prosperity'[93]. Later, she observes that, although the relation between shifting technologies and population is complex, 'Malthusian theory overlooks the effect of population increase on technological change.' and is simply 'unrealistic'[94].

Naturally, there is some discussion between these poles. Scientist Jared Diamond points out that, among the many societal collapses across history, there are still some 'success stories inspiring imitation and optimism', the lessons of which should teach us to 'live within our means.'[95] Economist Elinor Ostrom, whose work responds to Hardin's thought experiment, observes that a solution to overexploitation of resources may lie in local communities committing 'themselves to a cooperative strategy that they themselves will work out.'[96] Similarly, political scientist Thomas

---

[92] Nasong'o, Shadrack Wanjala, 'Environmental Policy and Practice in Kenya: Between Cornucopians and Neo-Malthusians', *The International Journal on Green Growth and Development*, 3(1), p3.

[93] Boserup, Ester, *The Conditions of Agricultural Growth: The Economics of Agrarian Change Under Population Pressure*, p86.

[94] Boserup, Ester, *Population & Technological Change: A Study of Long-Term Trends*, p5; Boserup, Ester, 'The Impact of Scarcity and Plenty on Development', *The Journal of Interdisciplinary History*, 14(2), p384.

[95] Diamond, *Collapse*, pp11, 531.

[96] Ostrom, Elinor, *Governing the Commons: The Evolution of Institutions for Collective Action*, p15.

Homer-Dixon foresees difficult times ahead, but acknowledges these challenges also present important opportunities – if we are able to take advantage of them[97].

On Ravolox, keeping population growth and natural resources in equilibrium is achieved through Drathro's meticulous husbanding of food and water. This balance is protected by culling the surplus population. From what we see of the near-execution of the Doctor, this awful measure is enacted by the Underground Dwellers themselves. Thus, Drathro's human workers are, in effect, a self-limiting population. Neo-Malthusians would see these circumstances, however dreadful, as simply one version of population management, a model of control not entirely uncommon amongst some societies. The Aché tribe of eastern Paraguay, for instance, are an indigenous people who practised a form of euthanasia as a survival mechanism[98]. In short, the L3's strategy is an application of Malthusian logic – cornucopian thinking, or Boserupian optimism, has no place in Marb Station. There is a point missing here, though. Drathro's survival chamber, for all intents and purposes, is a closed system. Within this sealed space, some form of Malthusian brake is essential in maintaining its fragile viability; a fragility that is entirely artificial. For, just a short distance from these living quarters, the now-recovered surface of Ravolox offers ample opportunity to recharge its food stocks, if only their so-called Immortal could move beyond its programming.

Cognitive constraints aside, it is possible that the condition of the

---

[97] Homer-Dixon, Thomas F, *The Upside of Down: Catastrophe, Creativity, and the Renewal of Civilization.*

[98] Harford, Tim, 'What Happens When We're Too Old to Be "Useful"?'

Underground Dwellers offers a continuum between Malthusian and Boserupian perspectives, reflecting those thinkers who argue that these vantage points are not entirely incompatible[99]. Whereas Malthus' theory prefigures Drathro's static reasoning, Boserup's vision of a rising population driving up productivity reflects the latent potential of the Underground Dwellers, only stymied by the closed condition of their survival chamber. To open this chamber would be to catalyse their potential. It is this blurring of Malthusian pessimism and Boserupian positivity which is seen in the Tribe of the Free, a society that echoes, albeit inadvertently, a more equal relation with the natural world.

The Good Life

Within walking distance of what was once London Underground's Marble Arch station, the Tribe of the Free lives as a forest-dwelling community, subsisting on the land. Its geographical positioning echoes those postapocalyptic stories, such as Walter M Miller Jnr's *A Canticle for Leibowitz* (1959), where seemingly secure urban spaces are upended by a civilisation-crushing event and replaced by small-scale settlements with repurposed technical resources. Not unlike Miller's classic, which describes the centuries after a world-changing episode, the Doctor's and Peri's visit to Ravolox takes place several hundred years after the visitation of the fireball. By this time, the Tribe of the Free is a functioning society, complete with authority figure (Queen Katryca), spiritual beliefs (multiple gods, including the Earth God Haldren) and a system of punishment (burnings), which

---

[99] Marquette, Catherine M, 'Turning but Not Toppling Malthus: Boserupian Theory on Population and the Environment Relationships', p12.

also applies to those so-called star travellers who threaten their precious totem (Drathro's black light converter aerial).

Considering its settled status, it appears reasonable to deduce that the Tribe of the Free is a largely agricultural society, whose people use hunter-gatherer practices to supplement their harvest. It also possesses an awareness of more advanced times, however. As Katryca herself puts it, defeating the Immortal will enable her people to rediscover 'the mysteries and treasures of our ancient forefathers'[100]. Yet, it is the application of these former technologies, with their cornucopian dimension, which has helped to transform much of today's natural world into a commodity; a process by which more than 70% of the Earth's land surface has been coopted for human use, whether for habitation or agriculture[101]. As such, it is difficult to envisage humanity as anything other than a grasping species, or as the political philosopher John Gray so uncompromisingly puts it, 'homo rapiens'[102].

In spite of this bleak diagnosis, some groups and individuals have long sought a less consuming and more materially equitable way of life, a little closer to the food production practices of the Tribe of the Free. These back-to-the-land movements directed their efforts towards building and maintaining less energy-intensive communities, where a balance might be struck between human and non-human needs; a sort of quasi-state of nature, but certainly not

---

[100] Part Three.

[101] England, Kate Arsac, 'How Human Activity Has Changed Earth's Land Surface'.

[102] Gray, John, *Straw Dogs: Thoughts on Humans and Other Animals*, p7.

Hobbesian[103]. Rather, it has a Heideggerian slant in its perspective on the world and its intention to dwell within it.

A starting point for these communities is the activism of the US lawyer Bolton Hall. In 1907, he wrote that, through brave application, one may possess property and 'acres of fruit and vegetables, flowers and poultry, and learn the best methods so as to insure success.' Hall's wider point, that urban dwellers yearn for 'the freedom of country life', is aimed at a self-sufficient lifestyle as much about political liberty as economic freedom[104]. This observation is echoed in Ravolox's surface dwellers, whose agrarian living is far from the comforts of an industrialised lifestyle, yet it is nonetheless free to grow and develop in ways which are impossible in the mechanical straitjacket of Drathro's domain.

Following the ideas of Hall, Ralph Borsodi's *This Ugly Civilisation* (1929) begins in a similarly emphatic style, critiquing the state of 1920s America in no uncertain terms. Published shortly before the Wall Street Crash, Borsodi's remarks prefigure the Doctor's equally frank comments on the state of civilisation in *The Mutants* (1972), where he tells Jo Grant of 'Grey cities linked by grey highways across grey deserts [...] Slag, ash, clinker. The fruits of technology.'[105] For Borsodi, seen by some as an 'agrarian idealist', the need for a social reset, driven by local ownership (see Borsodi's Law) and a renewed ethic of self-reliance, is as much about pushing back the frontiers of

---

[103] Hobbes, Thomas, *Leviathan*, pxix. In this classic work, Hobbes sets out his picture of human existence before a governing system is established, where 'the life of man, is solitary, poore, nasty, brutish and short.'

[104] Hall, Bolton, *Three Acres and Liberty*, p1.

[105] *The Mutants*, Episode One.

the state as it is establishing an ecological equilibrium[106].

Following a similar line of thought, Seymour's *The Complete Book of Self-Sufficiency* is replete with practical advice on everything from animal husbandry to foraging to making bricks[107]. In every sense it is a 'complete' guide to living off-grid. However, the groundwork for it appears in his earlier 1961 autobiography *The Fat of the Land*. In it, Seymour recounts his family's experience moving to a farm in Suffolk and practising techniques of self-sufficiency. Unlike the more ideological framings of Hall and Borsodi, Seymour's reflections describe a way of life that understands and recognises the value and interconnectedness of nature within a specific place. The Tribe of the Free exists within a similar model of understanding – albeit one where failure to harvest a good crop or forage enough wild food spells disaster. Thus, living within nature on such immediate and intimate terms may encourage a deeper respect for it; a respect built on the fundamental need to survive. It is this sort of awareness that moves us away from the sociopolitical aspects of these initiatives, and to a place where we may directly interact with the land – Scruton's 'act of settling' – and come to appreciate it in and of itself. For some, this particular cognisance of place is found in the ideals and concepts of ecologism.

---

[106] Issel, William H, 'Ralph Borsodi and the Agrarian Response to Modern America', *Agricultural History*, 41(2), p155. Borsodi's Law states that, while production costs decrease due to operational centralisation, distribution and processing costs increase disproportionately, hence the call for locally sourced goods.
[107] Seymour, John, *The Complete Book of Self-Sufficiency*.

Emerald Thinking

In terms of raw power consumption, our interaction with the non-human world has long been skewed in our favour. We are, simply put, the ecologically dominant species[108]. Efforts to soften this asymmetry have been limited. For every off-grid community, like Tinker's Bubble in Somerset and Brithdir Mawr in Pembrokeshire, there are settlements measured in the hundreds of millions, fed and watered by energy demanding processes[109]. As the Australian philosopher Arran Gare puts it, 'despite some local successes, globally, humanity is failing' – and Gray's homo rapiens is winning[110]. We are culturally influenced, too, at least in Western societies, by an entrenched anthropocentrism. From the Old Testament's proclamations on humanity as 'imago Dei', to Aristotle's rational animal, to René Descartes' view of animal life as no different from automata, the distinction between human and non-human beings has seldom been anything less than stark[111].

Although what we see of Drathro's survival chamber seems to do little to diminish this perspective, there may yet be green shoots, in the form of Balazar's enthusiasm for the worlds described in Marb Station's modest library. This attitude shows a potential for ecological care, at least on an individual level, as well as the power of the

---

[108] Tivy and O'Hare, *Human Impact on the Ecosystem*, pp32-34.
[109] Brace, Pedro, 'A Simple Woodland Life' *Reforesting Scotland*, (45); Howard, Sally, 'The Rise of Woodland Off-Gridders: "It Makes More Sense Than a Nine-to-Five"'.
[110] Gare, Arran, 'Internalizing Aldo Leopold's Land Ethic', *Cosmos and History: The Journal of Natural and Social Philosophy*, 17(3), p398.
[111] *Genesis* 1:27; Aristotle, *Nicomachean Ethics*, 13:1; Descartes, René, *A Discourse on the Method*, Part I.

written word to influence a receptive mind. The emergence of ecologism, with its ambition of rebalancing the dynamic between humanity and the natural world, is an example of this sense of care. Its advent in the middle years of the 20th century, in the shadow of newly-risen nuclear technology, is hardly coincidental. Still, as a discrete political thought, it may offer some traction in framing the apparently circular relationship between place and ecology, briefly sketched above.

Associated with the work of Arne Næss, EF Schumacher and Fritjof Capra, ecologism arose out of the powerful articulations of Aldo Leopold and Rachel Carson, amongst others. In *A Sand County Almanac* (released in 1949, the same year that the Soviet Union detonated its first nuclear weapon), Leopold argues for a new understanding of land: a land ethic, in fact. Specifically, if we no longer see land as a commodity – a Judaeo-Christian and Islamic framing – and instead 'as a community to which we belong, we may begin to use it with love and respect.'[112]

In a similar vein to Baker's *The Peregrine*, Leopold's *A Sand County Almanac* includes a series of essays set across the months of the year. In February, for instance, he explains that to avoid thinking that the grocer and the furnace are our providers of food and heat, we should plant a garden and harvest the wood ourselves[113]. Herein lies the central distinction between the Underground Dwellers and the Tribe of the Free: the former existing in separation from nature, the latter living as a part of it – and to be part of something, in Leopold's view,

---

[112] Gare, 'Internalizing Aldo Leopold's Land Ethic', p397.
[113] Leopold, Aldo, *A Sand County Almanac*, p6.

is to encourage care for it.

The ecological momentum set in motion by writers such as Leopold builds further in the work of Schumacher, whose *Small is Beautiful* (1973), with its frank subtitle *Economics as If People Mattered*, is one of ecologism's canonical texts. In it, the German-born economist argues for a scaling down of our ballooning economies, to bring about 'the convenience, humanity, and manageability of smallness.'[114] The key word here is 'humanity'. Finding humanity within modern economic processes is about recoupling the means of production with the natural cycles of the Earth's ecosystems. To do this, Schumacher adopts a Buddhist picture of economics, invoking the Noble Eightfold Path's 'Right Livelihood', a Buddhist practice which, if properly manifested, may help to humanise our modern economies[115].

In the same year that *Small is Beautiful* was first published, the Norwegian thinker Arne Næss articulated a more layered view of ecologism. He presents two levels of concern: deep ecology, which conceptualises nature as intrinsically valuable; and shallow ecology, which values the natural world on the basis of its utility to human beings[116]. The former refers to 'The well-being and flourishing of human and nonhuman life on Earth', a situation which, if realised, would mean establishing a very different world[117]. Næss' reference

---

[114] Schumacher, EF, *Small is Beautiful: Economics as If People Mattered*, p69.
[115] Schumacher, *Small is Beautiful*, p56.
[116] Næss, Arne, 'The Shallow and the Deep, Long-Range Ecology Movement: A Summary', *Inquiry: An Interdisciplinary Journal of Philosophy* 16(1-4).
[117] Næss, Arne, *There is No Point of No Return*, p2.

to 'flourishing', developed with writer George Sessions as part of the Deep Ecology Platform, is worth emphasising[118]. The term is viewed by some as a more precise translation of Aristotle's concept of the good life, 'eudaimonia'[119]. We may see, then, a crossover of sorts between the anthropocentrism of Aristotle and other Western thinkers, and the efforts of deep ecologists, such as Næss, to reimagine human-nonhuman relations.

Applying Schumacher's Buddhist economics and rethinking our relationship with the wider world, in line with Næss's deep ecology, is no mean feat. For some, it may seem little more than a fiction. In its way, Drathro's inability to move beyond its logical programming, and utilise the renewed surface of Ravolox, is not so dissimilar to the seemingly fossilised support which exists for today's consumer economy. Moving away from this consumptive model may prove as challenging as dismantling the anthropocentric thinking which has fired so much of human history. There could be another way, however. A route ahead which takes the naturalistic setting of the Tribe of the Free and blends it with the technological conditions of the Underground Dwellers, thus connecting to nature whilst also embracing elements of industrialised life – in Katryca's words, 'All the strange materials that bend and do not break' – so as to have the best of both worlds[120].

Individuals like John Seymour and low-impact communities like Tinker's Bubble have very likely already struck this balance. If so, it is a symmetry which may be further nourished by appreciating the

---

[118] De Jonge, Eccy, *Spinoza and Deep Ecology*, pp1-2.
[119] Kraut, Richard, 'Aristotle's Ethics'.
[120] Part Three.

circularity between place and ecologism.

Circular Simplicity

The care for place witnessed in communities like Tinker's Bubble is laudable. This is neatly captured in the 2021 documentary *Eve* by filmmakers Joya Berrow and Lucy Jane[121]. Berrow and Jane explore the experience of living off-grid from the perspective of Eve, a nine-year-old member of Tinker's Bubble, who faces the challenge of starting a new school whilst adopting a lifestyle far removed from that of her peers. Eve's attachment to the natural world is palpable. She is a devoted environmentalist (the documentary contains footage of her participation in a climate change rally in London, where she gives a rousing speech) and clearly possesses an acute awareness of the biosphere around her. Eve's care for the natural world is, perhaps, of a piece with Shepherd's 'journey into Being'[122]. One might even go so far as to argue that this mentality is the mindset of a place-aware and ecology-aware individual; a variation on environmental understanding which may be summarised in the Pagan figure of the Green Man[123].

This vital interplay between locational and ecological concerns exists in two particular Ravoloxians: Balazar and Broken Tooth. Each is on a journey of knowing, one as the Reader of the Books; the other as Queen Katryca's enforcer. Both are equally set within a complex web of spatial and environmental awarenesses. In the case of Balazar, this

---

[121] Berrow, Joya and Jane, Lucy, *Eve: The Off-Grid Life of a Nine-Year-Old Climate Activist*.

[122] Shepherd, *The Living Mountain*, p108.

[123] Also known as 'Jack in the Green', the Green Man is a Pagan symbol of rebirth, which signals the coming of spring after winter.

is seen in his bookish interest in the natural spaces which once existed beyond Marb Station. In Broken Tooth, it is his keen understanding of Ravolox's natural topography. Interestingly, the greenery into which Balazar and Broken Tooth escape is likely a good deal richer and more diverse than many of the woodlands extant in Britain today. Author Peter Fiennes points out that the remarkable biodiversity of an ancient woodland may need 'many hundreds of years' to properly establish[124]; a timescale which matches the period between the High Council's devastating translocation of Earth and the Doctor's investigations.

Within this wild and unspoilt space, understandings of place and ecology may meet, entwine and ultimately form a circular arrangement which feeds and extends both aspects. Balazar's understandings may be confined to words, and presumably pictures, but this does not diminish them. In the case of Balazar, these imaginative states range across zoological observation, fairytale adventuring and an epic hunt in ocean waters. Collectively, these works provide a rich mental tapestry with which to develop an awareness of the world, spatial and environmental. In contrast, Broken Tooth's above-ground life is one of subsistence survival. This includes the activity of hunting, which can prompt powerful mental states. The writer and environmentalist George Monbiot knows this firsthand. Whilst fishing from his kayak, some distance from shore, he writes that 'The wind ravelled through my mind, the water rocked me. Nothing existed except the sea, the birds, the breeze. My mind blew empty.'[125] Monbiot's observation is telling. It points to a

---

[124] Fiennes, Peter, *Oak and Ash and Thorn*, pp227-28.
[125] Monbiot, George, *Feral*, p16.

Buddhist-like experience, where the act of hunting transforms our mindscapes into a tabula rasa, receptive to the world beyond.

The worlds of Balazar and Broken Tooth echo another aspect of this circularity: both live on simple terms with their respective environments: one confined to a limited space where water and food are controlled, the other free to roam in search of sustenance. Thus, space and care for the environment (even one confined to an underground setting) are inextricably bound together. Moreover, these pared-back lifestyles, although enforced, still reflect the principles and practices of low-impact communities, themselves a variation on Schumacher's 'voluntary simplicity movement'[126]. In concert, their race memory of the fireball, the centuries of constraint, and the deep-rooted power of place to affect their perspective on nature, may bring about a more cautious, even mindful, interaction with the natural world. For Ravolox's surviving humans have the most extraordinary opportunity to begin again, on more equal terms with a largely regenerated world.

This final point is perhaps the most precious opportunity of all. As Monbiot writes, thriving ecosystems rely on complex diversity and a lack of disturbance (e.g. tree felling); a fact which is lost not only on those who see nature as a commodity, but also on some of today's conservationists[127].

---

[126] Schumacher Centre for New Economics, 'Schumacher on Buddhist Economics'.
[127] Monbiot, *Feral*, pp209-10.

CHAPTER 4: RAVOLOX, VOLITION AND THE MIND

Arranging place and ecology in a mutually beneficial relationship may offer a way into greater environmental sensitivity, and perhaps even a route towards Næss' deep ecology. Certainly, the worlds of Balazar and Broken Tooth offer some context regarding this kind of interaction. Although their traditions and technologies are divergent, their realities present an understanding of location and environment which may enter into a Heideggerian sense of care; one that complements Heidegger's sense of dwelling. Significantly, there is a further component to this arrangement. To give traction to the circularity of place and ecology, the power of personal volition (free choice) is required. It is this concept, in the context of the L3 robot, Drathro, and its prerequisite property, consciousness, which is explored here.

First, some words on volition. Cognitive freedom, or freedom of the mind, has occupied theologians and philosophers for millennia. For Christian thinkers, it is a key defence, or theodicy, to the existence of an all-powerful and all-loving God, in a world where evil exists. Conversely, British philosopher Galen Strawson argues that free choice cannot exist because to be ultimately responsible for how we are 'requires the actual completion of an infinite series of choices'[128]. Psychologists and neuroscientists have joined the fray, too, pouring quantitative and qualitative data on the question of volition, with conflicting results. The Libet experiments of the early 1980s, for

---

[128] Strawson, Galen, 'The Impossibility of Moral Responsibility', *Philosophical Studies*, 75(1-2), p7.

instance, which found that neural activity corresponding to simple movements (e.g. raising an eyebrow) registered several hundred milliseconds **before** the subject became conscious of the decision to move, are now critiqued by alternate positions, revealing the tangled nature of volition even in scientific circles[129].

The possibility of Drathro possessing cognitive freedom raises several hypothetical questions. First, if the L3 is free, then why is it so constrained by its programming that it resorts to using intellectually gifted humans to resolve its energy problems? This surely implies an innate lack of free will, which may point to a corresponding lack of consciousness. There again, if Drathro is little more than a clockwork automaton, why then is it so attached to its 'world' that it believes its human population, like the servants of some pharaoh, should not survive it? To answer these questions, we need to briefly trace the issue of consciousness, and whether a self-aware Drathro is capable of free choice.

To this end, we begin by considering the degree to which Drathro's cognitive powers represent consciousness, using the work of thinkers such as Gottfried Leibniz, Gilbert Ryle and John Searle. Extending this inquiry, we then turn to the concept of qualia, through the ideas of Thomas Nagel and Frank Jackson, amongst others. These vantage points may provide an initial outline of Drathro's mental state. Next, we explore whether Drathro experiences growth in an

---

[129] Libet, Benjamin, Gleason, Curtis A, Wright, Elwood W and Pearl, Dennis K, 'Time of Conscious Intention to Act in Relation to Onset of Cerebral Activity (Readiness-Potential): The Unconscious Initiation of a Freely Voluntary Act', *Brain*, 106(3); Clarke, Peter GH, 'The Libet Experiment and its Implications for Conscious Will.'

epistemic context. We then turn to Drathro's attempts to expand its apparent potential for learning. To finish, and assuming some level of consciousness and volition on the part of Drathro, we sketch the idea of freedom as a burden, using Jean-Paul Sartre's 'mauvaise foi' ('bad faith'), to offer some initial replies to the foregoing questions.

Drathro in the Chinese Room

Mechanical artefacts have a long history, extending from the Babylonian waterclock[130], to Charles Babbage's 'calculating engine'[131], to algorithm-powered chatbot technologies[132]. Whether driven by water, steam or electric-fired binary coding, none of the above is anything more than an intelligent device. The same can be said of Drathro, if we take its utterances and actions as only so much matter and energy in motion. Here, the German mathematician Gottfried Leibniz is worth noting. In Section 17 of his acclaimed 1715 work *The Monadology*, Leibniz describes how mental features, such as thought and perception, cannot be explained in material terms. He refers to a hypothetical machine, which can think, feel and perceive. Like a mill, it is large enough to enter and observe in some detail. However, such investigations would not yield evidence as to the nature of the machine's thought process, perception and

---

[130] Fermor, John and Steele, John M, 'The Design of Babylonian Waterclocks: Astronomical and Experimental Evidence', *Centaurus*, 42(3).
[131] Purbrick, Louise, 'The Dream Machine: Charles Babbage and His Imaginary Computers', *Journal of Design History* 6(1), p9.
[132] Deng, Jianyang and Lin, Yijia, 'The Benefits and Challenges of ChatGPT: An Overview', *Frontiers in Computing and Intelligent Systems*, 2(2).

otherwise[133]. Such qualities, for a rationalist like Leibniz, are beyond empirical study.

Does Leibniz's mill analogy, itself a strain of Cartesian dualism with its separation of mind and body, reduce Drathro to the status of an oversized calculator[134]? Not necessarily. Oxford scholar Gilbert Ryle refutes the Cartesian view. His efforts to dismantle Descartes' mind-body distinction – 'the myth of the ghost in the machine'[135] – see consciousness as explicable in behavioural terms, whereby 'mental events are logical constructions out of actual and possible behavior events.'[136] In short, there is no inner 'theatre' of mental events, only episodes of behaviour, manifested or dispositional, which are misconstrued as representations of mental phenomena[137]. For Drathro, Ryle's perspective might support claims of mental properties within its metallic frame, since if its behaviour and dispositions (e.g. attitudes, desires, intentions) broadly align with those of conscious beings, there may be weight to the argument that it too is a conscious being, albeit artificially conscious.

The L3's behaviour, at least regarding its own survival, seems to be more than just persistent programming at work. But could this

---

[133] Leibniz, Gottfried, *The Monadology and Other Philosophical Writings*, pp227-28.
[134] Cartesian dualism stems from the ideas of French philosopher René Descartes, who argued that mind and body are distinct substances, the former lacking extension, the latter existing in three-dimensional space.
[135] Ryle, Gilbert, *The Concept of Mind*, p62.
[136] Putnam, Hilary, 'Brains and Behavior', in Butler, RJ, ed, *Analytical Philosophy* vol 2, p25.
[137] Ryle, *The Concept of Mind*, p211.

determination be accountable solely on mechanical grounds? John Searle's Chinese Room thought experiment may throw some light on the matter. Searle describes a person in a locked room who receives written communications in the form of Chinese script from outside the room. Using a manual, and a collection of pre-made Chinese writings, the individual can reply to these messages and, for all intents and purposes, hold a conversation – despite having absolutely no knowledge of written Chinese. Hence, the perception of the person's behaviour from **outside** the room does not match the reality **within** the room. Searle's argument is that, despite the perception of intelligent behaviour, there is no actual understanding or equivalent mental state present, only a series of inputs and outputs[138].

The Chinese Room thought experiment attempts to counter arguments for hard artificial intelligence: the view that sufficiently advanced machines could think like humans. Alan Turing's 1950 paper 'Computing Machinery and Intelligence' prefigures this idea. In the opening section, titled 'The Imitation Game', Turing presents the idea that a machine's responses, in any given situation, might become indistinguishable from a human's[139], foreshadowing the concerns explored in fictional works, such as Ridley Scott's *Blade Runner* and its replicant-identifying Voight-Kampf test. It also begs a question: if Drathro could pass such a test, then would this demonstrate it possesses artificial consciousness?

---

[138] Searle, John R, 'Minds, Brains, and Programs', *The Behavioural and Brain Sciences* 3, pp417-18.

[139] Turing, Alan, 'Computing Machinery and Intelligence', *Mind* 49, pp433-35.

Sceptics of artificial intelligence systems developing self-awareness may refer to Searle's Chinese Room. They might conclude that this scenario, which denies computer processing systems emergent mental properties, represents Drathro's true condition. Certainly, from the Doctor's perspective, or Humker's and Tandrell's, the robot can express views, intentions and dispositions, but where is the evidence that it contains a subjective inner life? This is a difficult query to answer. Drathro's body is clearly mechanical, implying an arrangement of locomotive parts, circuits and other electrical components, not unlike a futuristic version of Leibniz's mill. But the matter of Drathro's desperate attempts to survive, and its obsession with its subterranean world, still loom large. Might these attitudes point to something over and above the purely material and discernible? If so, such intangibility puts this behaviour outside exclusively empirical metrics and squarely within the bounds of that rather unusual concept, qualia.

What Is It Like to Be Drathro?

Subjective experience, also known as qualia, is a curious thing. It refers to a private, mental world, which only the individual concerned can directly encounter. The mystery of this inner space is explored by the philosopher Thomas Nagel in his 1974 paper 'What Is It Like to Be a Bat?'. Here, Nagel states that 'fundamentally an organism has conscious mental states if and only if there is something that it is like to **be** that organism'. He further observes that no amount of reductive studying of mental phenomena can frame 'the subjective character of experience.'[140] If Nagel is correct,

---

[140] Nagel, Thomas, 'What Is It Like to Be a Bat?', *The Philosophical Review*, 83(4), p436 (author's emphasis).

then might not the puzzle of human consciousness extend to those artificial intelligences that exhibit similar behaviours? Drathro's struggle to maintain its black light supply may count as such an action and therefore an indication, however slight, of an inner mental world with a corresponding capacity for free will.

Like Nagel, philosopher of science Peter Godfrey-Smith argues that mental phenomena occur in a range of animals. However, he finds that Nagel's 'term 'like' is misleading' and that it is 'the feel of our lives' which is at the core of consciousness[141]. Is this where analysis of Drathro's mental status comes undone? For, unlike a human being, the experiential complexities of Drathro's cognition can surely be reduced to coils of coding and command lines, which in no way are like the intangible 'feel' which Godfrey-Smith describes. The nub of the matter rests on whether consciousness can be rationally quantified. Philosopher Colin McGinn is not convinced. Despite being clear on the question of consciousness existing, McGinn is not taken with the physical world as a carrier for consciousness. He argues that 'electrochemical impulses travelling along nerve strands seem far removed from what they somehow secure,' and that 'The operations of matter look like a singularly inadequate foundation for a mental life.'[142] Might this understanding apply equally well to alleged instances of artificial consciousness? After all, why should data processing in an organic brain be privileged over data processing in a synthetic brain?

Drathro's status as a self-aware entity depends on the answers to

---

[141] Godfrey-Smith, Peter, *Other Minds: The Octopus and the Evolution of Intelligent Life*, p78.

[142] McGinn, Colin, *Problems in Philosophy: The Limits of Inquiry*, p27.

these questions. However, without an objective explanation for the nature of consciousness, it remains inconclusive how this phenomenon could arise within a purely mechanical brain. Subjective mental properties – Godfrey-Smith's 'feel' of a life – reside outside the scope of scientific analysis, at least for the time being. In the philosophy of mind, these phenomena are called **qualia**, from the Latin, meaning 'of what sort' or 'of what kind' as in 'what kind of taste' or 'what kind of smell' and so forth. Frank Jackson's essay 'Epiphenomenal Qualia' (1982) addresses this concept through a thought experiment, generally known under the title 'Mary's Room'. Jackson describes a woman who has studied colour all her life, but who has no direct experience of it because she lives in an entirely black-and-white room. On leaving this room, Mary experiences colour for the first time. Jackson's argument here is that, despite Mary having a complete theoretical knowledge of colour, her first-person experience of colour **adds** to her learning, giving her an immediate and personal encounter, which cannot be defined or quantified. This additional sense data creates an experience which is an example of qualia. Jackson sums up the matter by stating that 'there are certain features of the bodily sensations especially, but also of certain perceptual experiences, which no amount of purely physical information includes.'[143]

If mental events, as directly experienced and interpreted by the individual, are beyond observable metrics, perhaps even pointing to some degree of cognitive closure, does this mean any analysis of Drathro's condition is equally opaque? Canadian philosopher Paul

---

[143] Jackson, Frank, 'Epiphenomenal Qualia', *The Philosophical Quarterly*, 32(127), p127.

Churchland disagrees on both counts. In challenging Nagel's and Jackson's arguments, Churchland claims that an understanding of mental states as readable physical states:

> 'will constitute not a gloom in which our inner life is suppressed or eclipsed, but rather a dawning, in which its marvellous intricacies are finally **revealed** – most notably, if we apply ourselves, in direct self-conscious introspection.'[144]

As an opponent of consciousness as a mysterious and unknowable thing, Churchland may offer us an alternative way into understanding whether Drathro possesses artificial consciousness. A fully computable conception of consciousness implies the possibility of manufacturing a similar condition within an artificial context. It seems not incredible, then, that Drathro, as the product of an advanced star-travelling civilisation, possesses mental phenomena in line with those events we take to be demonstrative of self-awareness.

Churchland's arguments do not go unanswered. Jackson later replies that when Mary first leaves her black-and-white room, she undergoes a learning experience, which cannot be theoretically replicated by following enough logical steps. Mary will also appreciate the mental life of others, such that when she 'sees her first ripe tomato, she will realise how impoverished her conception of the mental life of others has been all along.' Moreover, Jackson readily admits that his position does not rest on absolute proof, but nevertheless he maintains that it is plausible enough to refute

---

[144] Churchland, Paul M, 'Reduction, Qualia, and the Direct Introspection of Brain States', *The Journal of Philosophy*, 82(1), p28 (author's emphasis).

physicalist arguments[145].

Of course, this is far from being the end of things. In a later essay, titled 'Postscript on Qualia' (2004), Jackson begins to doubt the power of his thought experiment to defend these seemingly intangible phenomena, referring to it as an 'ingenious but flawed attempt to live with the unliveable.'[146] This being the case, and physicalist theories taking precedence in accounts of consciousness, then Drathro's status as a conscious being, as opposed to an intelligent but nonconscious machine, may yet be the more plausible explanation[147].

If Drathro is indeed self-aware, then it seems reasonable to conclude that, over the five centuries it rules the Underground Dwellers, it could undergo epistemic turns. By this, I mean that the L3 would probably acquire a growing bank of knowledge through specific experiential episodes. More simply put, Drathro would learn. So much so, in fact, that its mental states could become sufficiently altered as to entertain a level of executive function not unlike free will. We consider these epistemological episodes below, through Plato's Allegory of the Cave, and the concept of machine learning[148].

---

[145] Jackson, Frank, 'What Mary Didn't Know', *The Journal of Philosophy*, 83(5), pp291-5.

[146] Jackson, Frank, *Mind, Method and Conditionals: Selected Essays*, p67.

[147] Physicalist theories maintain that all mental events (e.g. consciousness) can be reduced to physical events.

[148] Epistemology is a branch of philosophy which explores the sources and limits of knowledge and involves questions such as 'How do I know what I know?'.

Epistemic Turns: Balazar and the Cave of Shadows

In his seminal work *The Republic*, Plato sets out the conditions for his ideal society. In exploring concepts such as justice and goodness, Plato uses an allegory, told through the figure of Socrates, to explain how knowledge is acquired. Typically referred to as the Allegory of the Cave, it tells of a group of prisoners kept in a subterranean space and chained in just such a way that they can only ever see what is immediately facing them. Behind them is a roadway and behind the roadway is a fire. In front of the prisoners is a wall. Unseen figures pass along the road, carrying raised up inanimate objects of various descriptions. The fire projects the silhouettes of these objects onto the wall. The prisoners think that what they see is reality. In fact, it is a shadow, as insubstantial as a will-o'-the-wisp and just as epistemologically dangerous. Eventually, one of the prisoners manages to escape. On reaching the surface, the escapee is dazzled by the power of the sun. In time, he becomes accustomed to the light and gradually perceives the actual world. Later, he returns to the cave, where he tries and recounts what has happened to him. However, his fellow prisoners do not believe a word of it. Still further, Socrates surmises that 'they would kill him who tried to release them and bear them up', such is their certainty that the world of the cave is reality and the escapee a mere fantasist[149].

The above summary attempts to outline the core idea of Plato's theory of knowledge. Namely, that the sensory world reflects the true reality, which is itself composed of mental templates, known as

[149] Plato, *The Republic*, 514a-517e.

the 'Forms' or 'Ideas', which sustain the physical copy. The escaped prisoner represents the individual who learns to see beyond the shadows and experience the perfection of the Forms. As such, Plato sees rational 'a priori' knowledge as superior (read more reliable) compared with empirical 'a posteriori' knowledge[150].

Balazar's experiences on Ravolox may well put him in the place of Plato's escaped prisoner, along with every other Underground Dweller who successfully joins the Tribe of the Free. Leaving behind the well-lit labyrinth of Marb Station and climbing the ruined stairway to the outside world, Balazar must confront a new reality; one in which the controlled and contained environ of the Immortal is exchanged for the sweeping vistas of Ravolox's surface. There may be some resonance here with Mary's Room (however much Jackson himself later critiques it), with Balazar's life below ground comparable to Mary's monochrome room, whilst his escape to the surface mirrors her own emergence and discovery of colour.

The epistemic journey on which Balazar embarks may indeed contain limited parallels to Plato's allegory. So, might the same be said of Drathro? After all, half a millennium of data processing surely amounts to something in epistemological terms, even something as quantifiable as machine learning. Certainly, the L3 can acquire knowledge of the world outside of its survival chamber (e.g., it knows precipitation has returned to the surface of Ravolox) and it is aware, logically at least, that some pre-fireball ecosystems (e.g., arboreal cover) are now in situ. Do these accumulative chunks of data

---

[150] A priori knowledge is drawn from theoretical reasoning (e.g., 2 + 2 = 4), whereas a posteriori knowledge is drawn from observation (e.g., Mercury is the closest planet to the Sun).

represent the potential for a radical change in Drathro's ratiocination? Put another way, would a certain store of data lead to a mental threshold which would lead to self-awareness?

The idea of epistemic events, however complex, catalysing the conditions for consciousness may be somewhat far-fetched; Plato's allegory entails an epistemological awakening, not a trigger for emergent self-awareness. Rather, there must also be an underlying neural architecture in place, which can feed off arising data like so much mental fertiliser, so as to create rational outputs which, in turn, circle round to shape inputs, and so on and so forth. The structure in question is likely to be a mix of hardware and software components that, together, can acquire, retain and retrieve blocks of information – life experiences, if you like – which then can be used to inform future actions. In short, an example of machine learning.

Epistemic Turns: Ravoloxian Ratiocinators

Epistemic changes, however significant or dramatic, are not sufficient in themselves to suggest a level of artificial intelligence bordering on artificial consciousness. There must, amongst other properties, be some demonstration of learning, too. A few words on machine learning may help to illuminate this point. In definitional terms, it 'focuses on developing algorithms that allow machines to improve their performance on a certain task over time through accumulating experiences.'[151] In Drathro's case, it is not immediately clear whether the L3 is equipped with such protocols. Its behaviour

---

[151] Shute, Valerie J, Fulwider, G Curt, Lui, Zhichun and Rahimi, Seyedahmad, 'Machine Learning', in Terney, Rob, Rizvi, Fazal and Ercikan, Kadriye, eds, *International Encyclopedia of Education* Volume 6, p84.

implies that it is unable to move beyond its programming (e.g., not accessing surface precipitation when it becomes available). Yet Drathro is able to seek out and act upon alternative modes of thinking. Specifically, it uses the mathematically gifted Humker and Tandrell to address its power source difficulties. Is there a contradiction here? And where does this leave us in terms of Drathro's learning capacity? In the first instance, these seemingly contradictory cognitive states still indicate an underlying logical coherence. In short, Drathro's failure to take advantage of a rainy Ravolox for the sake of its work units is perfectly consistent with its central purpose, i.e., maintaining a survival chamber for the Andromedan Sleepers and 500 'work units'. Equally, Drathro's efforts to resolve its looming power failure and maintain functionality are also compatible with its purpose. In the second instance, the L3 itself is quite clear on its ability to learn. Whilst coercing the Doctor into grappling with its black light error, it emphatically states, 'I have a learning capacity but my processors of ratiocination are logical.'[152]

So, Drathro is aware that its cognitive powers can be extended. But it is also cognisant of its rational limits. For whilst it is capable of learning, it cannot move beyond the coding of its programming without the assistance of 'organics' such as Humker and Tandrell, and later the Doctor. In some respects, this situation is not unlike our experience of consciousness, where there is a clear inner sense of our limitations, yet we are quite capable of looking for ways to cross these limits. Such defiance may indulge alternate mindsets, like poet John Keats' Negative Capability, where logic and reason are exchanged for non-rational phenomena that operate outside

[152] Part Two.

standard cognitive structures[153]. This echoes those strands of Eastern philosophy which draw on the ineffable, that is, properties which cannot be described in conventional terms. In *How the World Thinks* (2018), British philosopher Julian Baggini devotes a complete chapter to the concept. He observes that 'In Zen, language and rationality are both intellectual straitjackets', where language in particular 'adds to reality in that it creates an extra layer on top of it, and this in turn subtracts from reality by obscuring its fullness,' and 'Ultimate truth is beyond not just language but any rational understanding.'[154]

Drathro's engagement in unorthodox, if not ineffable, practices to overcome its challenges evidences its capacity for learning. This quality of discovery, and its place as regards consciousness, come to the fore in Axel Cleeremans' Radical Plasticity Thesis. According to Cleeremans, consciousness emerges out of a dynamic process, whereby awareness of inner mental conditions, and the emotional worth attached to this awareness, are manifested in those cognitive structures where learning takes place[155]. Put another way, consciousness is 'the brain's (emphatically non-conceptual) theory about itself, gained through experience interacting with the world,

---

[153] Gunderman, Richard, 'John Keats' Concept of "Negative Capability" – or Sitting in Uncertainty – is Needed Now More Than Ever'. Keats states that Negative Capability, first mentioned in a letter to his brothers in 1817, is 'when a man is capable of being in uncertainties, mysteries, doubts, without any irritable reaching after fact and reason'.

[154] Baggini, Julian, *How the World Thinks*, pp30, 32.

[155] Cleeremans, Axel, 'The Radical Plasticity Thesis: How the Brain Learns to be Conscious', *Frontiers in Psychology* 2, p1.

with other agents, and, crucially, with itself.'[156]

Cleereman's conjecture may resonate with aspects of Australian philosopher David Chalmers' idea of experience arising out of information. A leading figure in the field of consciousness studies, Chalmers writes that, if information is linked to experience, then where there is information there is experience, even in the case of very basic systems, such as the humble thermostat. In short, 'conscious experience is a realization of an information state'[157]. This being the case, Drathro is clearly an example of an information system. It is capable of acquiring, storing and manipulating quantities of data. So, following Chalmers' argument, if information does equate to experience, then Drathro possesses a capacity for experiential events. Following this, and if Drathro's behaviour does result from conscious properties rather than simply algorithmic programming, then Drathro also has the potential for free choice, itself a highly complex phenomenon.

Bad Faith in the Machine

In his paper 'How to Make a Mind', the futurist and computer scientist Ray Kurzweil concludes that, where the development of nonbiological brains is concerned, steps should be identified to educate such brains, starting with moral imperatives[158]. Kurzweil's observation on moral reasoning implies a degree of volition, a key

---

[156] Cleeremans, 'The Radical Plasticity Thesis', p4.

[157] Chalmers, David, 'Consciousness and Its Place in Nature', in Chalmers, David J, ed, *Philosophy of Mind: Classical and Contemporary Readings*, pp292-93.

[158] Kurzweil, Ray, 'How to Make a Mind', *The Futurist*, March-April 2013, p17.

factor not only in matters of ethics but in the exercise of justice systems, too[159]. Assuming Kurzweil's point in the case of Drathro, we find ourselves facing a number of ethical questions about the robot's actions. For example, the Andromedan Sleepers are long since dead by the time of the TARDIS's arrival on Ravolox. So why does Drathro persist in its routine? Is this where its programming comes to the fore? Perhaps not. Rather, the L3's behaviour speaks to a more subtle and complex motivation – an impulse which moves beyond ethics and into existentialism[160].

Existential philosophy has a number of contributors. However, as a school of thought, its principal architect is the 20th-century French playwright and philosopher Jean-Paul Sartre. His 1943 work *Being and Nothingness* is his most extensive exposition on the subject. In setting the groundwork of his philosophy, Sartre explores the concept of freedom and its critical place in the human condition. He writes that 'the essence of the human being is suspended in his freedom,' and 'Human freedom precedes essence in man and makes it possible'[161]. These are striking remarks. Sartrean 'essence' is the very purpose of things, and crucially human existence **precedes** it. According to this reading, freedom is the bridge between existence and purpose.

The matter of freedom, explains Sartre, contains an important caveat. There is a 'specific consciousness of freedom' and 'this

---

[159] Ludden, David, 'Can We Have Justice Without Free Will?'.
[160] A branch of philosophy which explores issues such as free will and living authentically.
[161] Sartre, Jean-Paul, *Being and Nothingness*, p25.

consciousness is anguish.'[162] But what is anguish? Enigmatically enough, Sartre refers to it as 'my consciousness of being my own future'[163]. In other words, our sense of our own freedom may be so overwhelming as to be a burden; a burden which some of us might choose to discharge by way of a comportment which Sartre calls 'mauvaise foi', typically translated as 'bad faith'. Sartre defines bad faith as 'a lie to oneself', which represents a transcendent action, through which 'it is from myself that I am hiding the truth.' This paradoxical state is summed up in the proposition, 'I must know in my capacity as deceiver the truth that is hidden from me in my capacity as the one deceived.'[164]

Sartre's understanding of freedom is nothing if not complex. At its root is bad faith, an inescapable aspect of consciousness[165]. Drathro, a machine fixated on an obsolete task, may be a prime example of it. First, it is wilfully blind to the changes which have unfolded on Ravolox, whether these be the regeneration of the planet's surface vegetation, the return of its water cycle, or the breathability of its air. Instead, the robot opts to continue with its overarching purpose, heedless of the growing evidence to the contrary. Is this not Drathro 'hiding the truth' from itself? Second, it persists in its obsession to maintain a survival chamber rendered irrelevant by the loss of the Sleepers. Does this not point to one who is in a state of self-denial, or rather bad faith? Third, Drathro's desperation to remain functional, even to the point of utterly dismissing Ravolox's human survivors, propels its 'processors of ratiocination' to deny the value

[162] Sartre, *Being and Nothingness*, p33.
[163] Sartre, *Being and Nothingness*, p32.
[164] Sartre, *Being and Nothingness*, pp48-49.
[165] Sartre, *Being and Nothingness*, p70.

of the Underground Dwellers, who it has managed and controlled for centuries. Surely, whatever the relationship between the L3 and its human workers, the idea that they can be so easily abandoned must infringe some part of its original programming? Here, a fugue-like state appears to point to Drathro running away from both itself and the very powers of volition which emerge from its status as a conscious being.

Hence, as if some sort of philosophical sleight of hand had been performed, we might suggest that, given how Sartrean ideas of volition seem to point to Drathro exhibiting behaviours associated with free will, which in turn presuppose some level of consciousness, artificial or otherwise, Drathro is indeed a self-aware machine intelligence with a singular personality. No wonder it is so terribly stubborn, or rather, in the Doctor's words, an 'Inflexible little fellow.'[166]

---

[166] Part Two.

CHAPTER 5: RAVOLOX AND IDENTITY

Previously, we explored understandings of place and Heidegger's idea of dwelling, in the context of Ravolox and its inhabitants. These points catalysed ecological concerns, looked at through the characters of Broken Tooth and Balazar. From here, we briefly turned to conceptions of consciousness and free will, using Drathro as a limited case study. This led us to the concept of bad faith, as presented in the work of Jean-Paul Sartre, and the highly tentative conclusion that volition is linked to representations of personal identity. Following this line of thinking, in this final chapter, we consider matters arising from personal identity.

Any survey of personal identity first involves examining the concept in isolation. Etymologically, 'identity' stems from the Latin word 'idem' and later 'identitas', meaning 'same'[167]. Similarly, the 17th-century English philosopher John Locke conceives it as 'participation of the same continued life' and argues that 'Consciousness makes personal identity' and without it 'there is no person.'[168] Locke goes on to state that consciousness allows personal identity to reach into the past, marking out memory as a factor in psychological – read, personal – continuity[169]. Locke's point, that consciousness, with its capacity to transcend the present and step into the past, is critical to personal identity, will have some bearing on an understanding of

---

[167] Qazimi, Shukran, 'Sense of Place and Place Identity', *European Journal of Social Sciences Education and Research*, 1(1), p248.
[168] Locke, John, *An Essay Concerning Human Understanding*, pp315, 319, 329.
[169] Locke, *An Essay Concerning Human Understanding*, p331; Baggini, Julian, *The Ego Trick*, p49.

Drathro.

Lockean ideas, first articulated in the late 1600s, continue to shape conceptions of personal identity to the present day. They are not without contrast, however. The philosopher David Hume can find no trace of a fixed and persisting identity. He asks from what impression or other this phenomenon arises, yet can find no such 'impression constant and invariable.' Pressing further, Hume observes that when he looks within himself, he invariably strikes upon perceptions, such as heat and light, but 'I never can catch myself at any time without a perception.'[170] In short, 'there is no experiencer.'[171] He goes on to argue that we are simply a 'bundle or collection of different perceptions, which succeed each other with an inconceivable rapidity, and are in a perpetual flux and movement.'[172] This hypothesis, often referred to as bundle theory, describes personal identity or selfhood as exclusively composed of properties or relations (e.g. perceptions) and is inconceivable without reference to them[173]. There is no core element, no 'pearl at the heart of our identity'[174].

Even a cursory look at Hume's arguments lies beyond this brief chapter. Still, it is important to recognise the challenge he raises to our traditional understandings of personal identity. Put simply, the bundle theory may reduce it to a sort of psychological illusion. To illustrate this point, let us consider the myth of Theseus' ship.

---

170 Hume, David, *A Treatise of Human Nature*, pp251-52.

171 Blackmore, Susan and Troscianko, Emily, *Consciousness: An Introduction*, p438.

172 Hume, *A Treatise of Human Nature*, p252.

173 Baggini, *The Ego Trick*, pp119-21.

174 Baggini, *The Ego Trick*, p72.

Accounts of this thought experiment on the continuity of identity appear in the works of Plato and Plutarch, as well as in the writings of Thomas Hobbes[175]. Hume references it more generally, amongst other thinkers[176]. Essentially, the myth centres on a wooden vessel, which over time is repaired until not one original piece of timber remains (not unlike the story of Trigger's broom, discussed below). So, given its complete physical change, is it the same ship? Extending the thought experiment, Hobbes describes a man collecting all the ship's worn-out parts and reassembling them[177]. There are now two ships, but which one is the ship of Theseus? Bizarrely, this brings us to the notion that **both** ships could be Theseus' ship. Hobbes dismisses the idea, but remarks that 'the beginning of individuation is not always to be taken either from matter alone, or from form alone.'[178]

It seems then that personal identity goes beyond purely physical arrangements, whether in terms of substance or appearance. Julian Baggini concurs here. He argues that whereas our physical and psychological aspects are important to our conception of selfhood,

---

175 Scaltsas, Theodore, 'The Ship of Theseus', *Analysis*, 40(3), pp153-54; Martínez de Arbulo, Alejandro, 'The Ship of Theseus: A Misleading Paradox? The Authenticity of Wooden Built Heritage in Japanese Conservation Practice', *Journal of Architectural Conservation*, 29(2), p152; Sedley, David, 'The Stoic Criterion of Identity', *Phronesis*, 27(3), p258.

176 Hume, *A Treatise of Human Nature*, p257; Giles, James, 'The No-Self Theory: Hume, Buddhism, and Personal Identity', *Philosophy East and West*, 43(2), p180.

177 Hobbes, Thomas, *The Collected Works of Thomas Hobbes*, pp136-137.

178 Hobbes, *The Collected Works*, p137.

they are not where our identity is housed. Moreover, since there is no locatable 'I' in a physical sense, and Baggini also denies the existence of a soul, we are left with the view that who we are, at bottom, is a construction[179]. It is our ability to see this assembly of pieces as a unified self, writes Baggini, rather than a collection of discrete parts, that becomes what he calls the Ego Trick[180]. He summarises his position in the line '**we are no more than, but more than just, matter**', a useful conception of personal identity to which we will adhere, going forward[181].

As before, this chapter is divided into parts, each focused on a particular feature of personal identity. Starting where the previous chapter left off, our opening focus is on continuity of identity in the form of Drathro. This is followed by an outline of collective identity through the circumstances of the Underground Dwellers and the Tribe of the Free, which includes the work of sociologist Richard Jenkins and asks whether collective framings of self are more resilient than individual ones. Next, we look at identity as a psychological construction in the figure of Merdeen, an Underground Dweller who lives a double life, first as a loyal servant of the Immortal and second as an agent of freedom. The research of clinical psychologist Ursula Wilder and political scientist Tom Lundborg is referenced in this section. Lastly, in an effort to circle back to our opening thoughts on this adventure, we return to the work of Yi-Fu Tuan and Edward Relph, along with sociologists Lee Cuba and David M. Hummon, with the aim of tying, however

---

[179] Baggini, *The Ego Trick*, p114.
[180] Baggini, *The Ego Trick*, pp119-23.
[181] Baggini, *The Ego Trick*, pp123-24 (author's emphasis).

tangentially, understandings of place to understandings of identity, by exploring the unique situation of Ravolox vis-à-vis its previous existence elsewhere as Earth.

Robots and Brooms

Am I the same person today as I was yesterday? Will I be the same person tomorrow as I was today? These questions find relevance in the aforesaid paradox of the ship of Theseus. There is resonance, too, in Steven Moffat's script *Deep Breath* (2014). Here, the Doctor compares the Half-Face Man, a cyborg who has substituted its worn-out parts for new, to a broom that has had its brush and handle replaced multiple times. Moffat's nod to the persistence of identity may owe something to the scene in **Only Fools and Horses** where the character of Trigger, a road sweeper, claims he has used the same broom for some 20 years – despite getting through 17 brush heads and 14 handles[182].

For Drathro, persistence of identity pivots on the robot's considerable lifespan. From what we are told, the L3 has been extant since at least the visitation of the fireball, some 500 years before the events involving the Doctor and Peri. This longevity, which may extend to before its mission to protect the Sleepers of Andromeda, is surely the reason behind the Underground Dwellers referring to it as the Immortal. As such a long-lived being, it seems reasonable to suppose that Drathro experiences wear and tear, which necessitates episodes of repair. On this point, Drathro tells the Doctor that it is trained in 'installation and maintenance,'[183] indicating that it can

---

[182] **Only Fools and Horses,** *Heroes and Villains* (1996).
[183] Part Two.

manage this process, whilst implying that its body has undergone substitutions á la Theseus' ship and Trigger's broom.

Like the traditional rebuilding of Japan's Grand Shrine of Ise every 20 years,[184] identity over time is at the heart of the matter here. Moreover, the case of Drathro is far from being the only fictive example. Jules Verne plays on the same conceit in his 1872 novel *A Fantasy of Dr Ox*, where he describes a lasting knife due to 'the endlessly repeated operation... of replacing the handle when it is worn out and the blade when it has lost its edge.'[185] The story of 'My Grandfather's Axe' follows a similar pattern, where the owner of the axe asserts that 'it has occasionally required some repairs. My father replaced the handle and I replaced the head.'[186]

This is where continuity of identity comes into focus, as we pose the two questions at the head of this section to the figure of Drathro. So how would the L3 answer them? First, if Drathro possesses a level of consciousness comparable to a human being, and a similar level of volition, its replies would likely mirror our own. After all, why should a self-aware being, with the capacity for free choice, be any less certain of its lasting identity because its body is comprised of metal and plastic rather than flesh and blood? Second, in the same way that human beings undergo mental and physical changes throughout their lives, surely Drathro's 'maintenance' entails a comparable, if

---

[184] Rambelli, Fabio, 'Floating Signifiers: The Plural Significance of the Grand Shrine of Ise and the Incessant Re-signification of Shinto', p230.

[185] Verne, Jules, *A Fantasy of Dr Ox*, p9.

[186] Hud, Nicholas V, Cafferty, Brian J, Krishnamurthy, Ramanarayanan and Williams, Loren Dean, 'The Origin of RNA and "My Grandfather's Axe"', *Chemistry & Biology*, 20(4), p466.

less subtle, series of alterations.

These points notwithstanding, we are left with the question of what, if anything, remains of Drathro as it exchanges one body part for another, perhaps substituting all of its physical components over the course of the five centuries it rules the Underground Dwellers. To answer this, let us think about Drathro's circumstances from the standpoint of Hume's bundle metaphor. Pursuing this, we may find ourselves tacking in the direction of Baggini's Ego Trick and our apparent capacity to retain a sense of 'I' amidst an ever-shifting sea of perceptions. Certainly, Drathro's situation seems not so far removed from our own, so why not refer to a similar answer? After all, rejecting this solution on the grounds that Drathro's maintenance involves major bouts of change rather than gradual adjustments, seems at best churlish and at worst prejudiced. Additionally, to recognise that Drathro's identity, like human identity, can endure over time, is to give the L3 robot a status which helps to explain its attempts to cling to life at any cost, an attitude it shares with most, if not all, sentient creatures.

Thus far, it appears that personal identity lies not only in a sort of self-deception, but also in the plain fact of our continuing existence across time. Longevity, then, offers another layer to our sense of self. Crucially, it is a form of personal survival made possible through our power of recall. Locke acknowledges this point in his story of a cobbler and a prince, whose souls exchange bodies but remain defined by the memories they carry with them into their new physical casings[187]. Heidegger also highlights the place of memory,

[187] Locke, *An Essay Concerning Human Understanding*, p324.

calling it no less than 'the gathering of thought.'[188] Selfhood, then, emerges from a coming together of recollections, which we tend to see as fixed and permanent, in the manner of Baggini's Ego Trick.

If we deny Drathro these elements of personal identity, what are the grounds for our own sense of self? A conscious machine that undergoes transformative events not unlike a person's growth and decline, and which possesses longevity and memory, surely warrants the status of possessing personal identity – however many broom handles and broom heads it may have had in its lifetime[189]. What is more, if we take these pieces as distinct **and** integral to Drathro's sense of self, we may approach the question of how identity can manifest and endure within a collective setting, such as a tribal group or community. The Tribe of the Free and the Underground Dwellers are examples of this emergent quality.

Tribal Dwellers

The complexities apparent in personal identity are no less evident in collective identity. Indeed, aspects of personal identity, such as ethnicity and gender, involve collective identities too[190]. Here, collective identity can be viewed as 'an individual's cognitive, moral, and emotional connection with a broader community, category, practice, or institution.' one which is 'expressed in cultural materials'[191] such as clothing. Whether these collective identities belong to recognised groupings or spontaneous gatherings, each one

---

[188] Heidegger, Martin, *What Is Called Thinking?*, p3.
[189] Sedley, David, 'The Stoic Criterion of Identity', p259.
[190] Jenkins, Richard, *Social Identity*, p103.
[191] Polletta, Francesca and Jasper, James M, 'Collective Identity and Social Movements', *Annual Review of Sociology*, 27, p285.

delineates boundaries within which identity arises. These limits develop out of group members sharing a common connection, conceptual or experienced,[192] which 'entails exclusion, if only by default.'[193] Some groups may be more or less exclusive than others. However, to operate as a discrete entity there must be some element of marking off, which can emerge over time or more quickly established, according to circumstance.

In Ravolox's overground and underground communities, group identity founded on common ground is evident in their respective situations. This is unsurprising given the value of community to collective identity[194]. Amongst the Underground Dwellers, for example, a standard uniform appears to be the norm, with Balazar and his fellows dressed in what is at best utilitarian apparel, and which is still seen in ragged form on Broken Tooth. This visual marker may seem superficial, but it helps to reinforce a bond which already exists between Drathro's workers. Theirs is a survivalist community, driven by an unseen and unquestioned controller, who tethers their existence to the bare essentials of life. They possess a fabricated history, built around a handful of written texts and a centuries-old catastrophe narrative. This lends their world a sense of coherence and naturally gives way to a strictly bounded understanding of a collective self. Likewise, the Tribe of the Free is survivalist in essence with a top-down authority structure. Its members work the land and share in a common awareness of the natural environment. For coherence, the Tribe maintains an established religion, offering an

---

192 Polletta and Jasper, 'Collective Identity and Social Movements', *Annual Review of Sociology*, 27, p285.

193 Jenkins, *Social Identity*, p102.

194 Jenkins, *Social Identity*, p133.

explanation to the visitation of the fireball, as well as a sense of meaning to an otherwise unforgiving existence.

Within these groups there are also individual identities. Balazar's role as Reader of the Books and Merdeen's as leader of the train guard reveal social identities[195]. Queen Katryca occupies a very specific command role, directing individual needs alongside those of the community. Such a meeting of needs brings with it challenges. One such dilemma entails a conflict between self-interest and the needs of the group[196]. In the case of the Underground Dwellers, an example of this collision is the water thief, who places their desires ahead of those of the community. Above ground, monogamy, given how few women are in the Tribe of the Free, would perhaps occupy a similar scenario. Sidestepping this dilemma through a strict rule of law is one solution. To this effect, both societies practice capital punishment, meted out by established justice systems, albeit ones far from transparent in their workings.

Despite these commonalities, the framings of these two collective identities are case-hardened by their differences. The Underground Dwellers, for instance, provide a recruitment resource for the Tribe of the Free, as shown in the work of Merdeen. Queen Katryca also seeks to usurp the Immortal and steal its technologies. In turn, Drathro's response to discovering that there are work units 'out of control, outside the plan,' is to dispatch the L1 service robot to

---

[195] Stets, Jan E, and Burke, Peter J, 'Identity Theory and Social Identity Theory', *Social Psychology Quarterly*, 63(3), p225.

[196] Krasny, Marianne E, *Advancing Environmental Education Practice*, p151.

'destroy the traitors.'[197] These hostile stances demonstrate oppositional identities, whereby each group can only flourish at the expense of the other. The extent of these boundaries also raises the question of whether collective identity is more resilient than individual identity. Collective identities certainly have the potential to persist far longer than an individual identity. They may also resist damage and loss if the structures underpinning them are sufficiently robust. These arrangements of social capital include shared values, traditions and customs, which give their members a powerful sense of belonging. What we see of the Underground Dwellers and the Tribe of the Free indicates they possess reserves of this social capital, built up over the many years of their struggles. But can such communal qualities enter into the identities of their individual members? The character of Merdeen, who operates under more than one identity, may offer us some insight here.

Manufacturing Merdeen

Merdeen is an unusual Underground Dweller. Ostensibly, he heads up the security detail of Marb Station, an armed detachment known as the train guard. He reports directly to the Immortal and has the authority to dispense justice on the Immortal's behalf. To all appearances, Merdeen is a reliable factotum, whose first interactions with the Doctor confirm this impression. In truth, this hardy figure selects Underground Dwellers to escape their subterranean confinement and join the Tribe of the Free, as Broken Tooth once did, and Balazar later does.

Merdeen's rationale for his actions is simple and reflects one of the

[197] Part Three.

key motivators for those drawn into spycraft[198]. When asked by Balazar why he risks his life, he replies, 'I am sick of the cullings.'[199] This powerful impulse is the determining factor in Merdeen's decision to subvert his position and become a double agent. In doing so, he masks his true intentions so that he can continue serving the Immortal and exploit his authority amongst his community. It is a choice which involves living under two identities, however. First, as Merdeen of the train guard, an unswervingly loyal servant to the Immortal in his castle. Secondly, as Merdeen the traitor, a plotter against an age-old tyrant.

Historically, the fictional concept of the covert agent dates back at least as far as the writings of Homer, and in particular the hero Odysseus, who, in the *Iliad*, is tasked with entering the Trojan camp undetected in order to acquire vital intelligence[200]. Later examples include Baroness Orczy's Scarlet Pimpernel, whose clandestine efforts to save France's aristocrats during the French Terror are not so very far away from Merdeen's. Managing this dual-identity lifestyle, however, affects the subject's sense of self. According to Ursula Wilder, a clinical psychologist with experience of the US intelligence community, the moment an individual passes on classified information they initiate a secret new identity that entails 'concealment, compartmentation, and deception.' This experience may be invigorating and diverting, but it might also be 'draining and

---

[198] Wilder, Ursula M, 'The Psychology of Espionage', *Studies in Intelligence*, 61(2), p20.
[199] Part Two.
[200] Wilder, Ursula M, 'Odysseus, the Archetypal Spy', *International Journal of Intelligence and CounterIntelligence*, 34(4).

stressful.'[201] For Merdeen, these challenges are evidenced in his decision to save the Doctor, an alien he has only recently encountered, at the cost of killing Grell, a train guard subordinate long known to him and who he had hoped to one day send to the Tribe of the Free. Such choices are fraught with psychological risk, however much they save lives. Thus, Merdeen's life as a double agent is a case of the means justifying the ends, however much those means weigh heavily upon him.

Merdeen's experience of leading distinct lives would not necessarily be unique within his community. Living within a surveillance-controlled society, such as Drathro's survival chamber, could create 'double lives insofar as we are subjects under scrutiny, our identities dispersed in a vast network of social relations, state records and material objects'[202]. As such, the environmental conditions in which the Underground Dwellers live could create dual identities for them all, emphasising the liberty of living above ground, where there is no such monitoring.

The end of this surveillance through Drathro's demise represents another turn in Merdeen's identity. With his struggle against the Immortal over, Merdeen faces re-embracing the part of his personality that he has been forced to conceal. This is unlikely to be a quick and easy business. Rather, it can entail significant psychological reconditioning. This is because maintaining his false

---

[201] Wilder, 'The Psychology of Espionage', p19.

[202] Czemiel, Grzegorz, '"Brought Up to Live Double Lives": Intelligence and Espionage as Literary and Philosophical Figures in Ciaran Carson's *Exchange Place* and *For All We Know*', *Text Matters: A Journal of Literature, Theory and Culture*, 11, p37.

identity as a faithful servant of the Immortal is not unlike what the British double agent Kim Philby refers to as a 'cover personality'. This element of a double agent's armoury gives authenticity to their cover story, but may become so impervious to detection that it is no longer possible to tell which personality is the real one[203]. In the case of Merdeen, there is no discernible fake persona, but certainly there is serious concealment of purposes, such that shedding the false impression Merdeen has long created will not be without challenge.

Finding room, as it were, in his new lifestyle, to reflect upon the past in a safe fashion and look towards the future with hope, will be part of the recovery process[204]. In this way, Merdeen might obtain what the French writer Albert Camus, in his reading of the myth of Sisyphus, calls the 'breathing space'. This is where the legendary prisoner-king, in returning to the foot of the hill up which he must endlessly push a boulder, becomes so utterly aware of his world that he is 'superior to his fate.' and 'stronger than his rock.'[205]

The Earth-Ravolox Conjunction

Earlier, we outlined how personal identity can endure despite change, referring to Baggini's Ego Trick concept and the figure of Drathro. A less obvious example of identity persisting through transformative events centres not on an individual, or object, but a place. This takes us back to the concept of place raised above. The

---

[203] Lundborg, Tom, 'Secrecy and Subjectivity: Double Agents and the Dark Underside of the International System', *International Political Sociology*, 15, pp449-50.
[204] The UK mental health charity Mind includes 'Take Notice' in its '5 Ways to Wellbeing'.
[205] Camus, Albert, *The Myth of Sisyphus*, p117.

location in question is Ravolox and our focus is its journey from displaced Earth to mysterious planet.

However, before considering Ravolox, we should define place identity, so as to put in situ some points which will later bear on Ravolox's condition. US psychologist Harold Proshansky is generally regarded as introducing the concept of place identity and defines it as 'those dimensions of self that define the individual's personal identity in relation to the physical environment[206]. Equally, sociologists Lee Cuba and David Hummon frame place identity as 'an interpretation of self that uses environmental meaning to symbolize or situate identity.'[207] Building on these conceptions, Richard Jenkins, an academic in the field of sociology, remarks that identification is relative to space, although whereas individual identity is embodied in different modes of being (e.g. physical, fictive, virtual), collective identity emerges out of location[208]. Features of place (e.g. settlements) also contribute to place identity and, by extension, personal identity[209]. In addition, connecting 'behavior and experience of the individual to his physical setting'[210] is key. As a

---

[206] Peng, Jianchao, Strijker, Dirk and Wu, Qun, 'Place Identity: How Far Have We Come in Exploring Its Meanings?', *Frontiers in Psychology*, 11, p1.

[207] Cuba, Lee and Hummon, David, 'A Place to Call Home: Identification with Dwelling, Community, and Region', *The Sociological Quarterly*, 34(1), p112.

[208] Jenkins, *Social Identity*, p48.

[209] Hull, R Bruce IV, Lam, Mark and Vigo, Gabriela, 'Place Identity: Symbols of Self in the Urban Fabric', *Landscape and Urban Planning*, 28, p110.

[210] Proshansky, Harold M, 'Theoretical Issues in Environmental Psychology', *The School Review*, 82(4), p551.

qualification to the above, Jenkins, referring to the work of British social anthropologist Anthony Cohen, observes that where communities face increasing change (e.g. political centralisation) 'boundaries of place and locality become less important'[211].

Whether locational boundaries are influential, it seems clear that there is a link between individual and collective identities on the one hand and place identity on the other. So where does this leave Ravolox? The effects of its translocation, it seems, include the loss of large numbers of its human population. What boundaries of place remain, at least in what was once London, are the product of an alien robot and a small quasi-medieval community. However modest in size, the interaction of these groups with their corresponding environments necessarily involves place identity, which in turn informs individual and collective conceptions of self, as well as encouraging positive attitudes towards environment and others[212].

What sort of place identity is present on Ravolox? As a world remade by external agency, the matter of how its past impinges on its present is important. The issue is particularly germane because of the relationship between longevity and the meaning of place[213]. Drathro's centuries-old survival chamber, the settlement of the Tribe of the Free, and the millennia-old human civilisations predating Earth's displacement, are all temporal anchors in Ravolox's place identity. Significantly, it is the human component, overground and underground, which gives substance to these moorings. This is because place identity tends to be 'socially mediated' and 'shaped

---

[211] Jenkins, *Social Identity*, p138.

[212] Peng, Strijker and Wu, 'Place Identity', p12.

[213] Cuba and Hummon, 'A Place to Call Home, p115.

by people's interpretations of place.'[214] Without a continuous population, in possession of a shared history, place identity may become severed from earlier understandings. Thus, the settlement of the Tribe of the Free would have little or no association with Ravolox's pre-fireball origins. In contrast, the survival chamber occupying a former piece of London transport infrastructure may yet be joined with its earlier iteration, and act as a sort of ancestral bridge between pre-fireball humanity and the Tribe of the Free. As Tuan points out, some places endure 'through eons of time, outliving the patronage of particular cultures.'[215] Lasting objects, like the Avebury henge and stone circles in Wiltshire and the Longstone megalithic monument on the Isle of Wight, are instances of what we might call persistence of place; their significance bound up in form, functionality and representation[216]. Hence a thread, however tenuous, may run between Marble Arch Underground station with its countless commuters and the world of the Underground Dwellers – a connection given still more weight in the memories of Drathro, which might well have survived the robot's destruction; recordings to add to Balazar's library, perhaps.

The Tribe of the Free might not have a clear throughline to their planet's earthly past, but there is an awareness of 'the mysteries and treasures of our ancient forefathers,' which may help forge a sense of place identity through time[217]. This knowledge is further tied to the Tribe's worship of the Earth God Haldren, through a remarkable totem that surely predates their emergence as a community.

---

[214] Cuba and Hummon, 'A Place to Call Home', pp126-27.
[215] Tuan, *Space and Place*, p163.
[216] Relph, *Place and Placelessness*, p61.
[217] Part Three.

Moreover, through a combination of the totem's history and function as a place of worship, this device goes beyond particular cultural meanings by possessing 'both general and specific import.'[218]

Where we circle back to the concepts outlined in earlier chapters is in the argument that place identity 'may be a subset of sense of place in that it influences peoples' connectedness or relatedness to place.'[219] If so, it highlights the concept of place as a 'complex ensemble – rooted in the past and growing into a future'[220]. This temporality returns us to Locke's argument for consciousness through memory offering continuity to personal identity. Perhaps the same may be said for place identity, whereby it is the history of place, however tangled and complicated, which sustains its identity across time, emphasising the value of linking Ravolox to its terrestrial heritage. On this point, Tuan writes that Earth is 'the human home in the cosmic scheme of things,' and that place – which includes understandings of 'home' – is a 'construct of experience,' maintained not only by material substance 'but also by the quality of human awareness.'[221] It is this sentience of place, which leads us into matters of place identity, and its practical effects on our lives.

---

[218] Tuan, *Space and Place*, p164.
[219] Hull, Lam and Vigo, 'Place Identity', p118.
[220] Tuan, Yi-Fu, 'Space and Place: Humanistic Perspective', in Gale, Stephen and Olsson, Gunnar, eds, *Philosophy in Geography*, p388.
[221] Tuan, Yi-Fu, 'Place: An Experiential Perspective', *Geographical Review*, 65(2), p165.

POSTSCRIPT: RAVOLOX AND PLACEHOOD

A sense of place entails different qualities. These can be categorised by person (e.g. individuals, groups), psychological processes (e.g. behaviour) and place (e.g. social, physical) and include notions of personal identity, consciousness, ecological concern, dwelling and topophilia[222]. Of these, dwelling is not only the more conceptually demanding but also the more central. In Heidegger's enigmatic prose, it is realised where we 'think for the sake of dwelling' and may be **the** factor in our obtaining lives of quiet, if not comprehended contentment[223].

Dwelling encapsulates the other qualities entailed in place. It also encompasses rootedness, a state of being which Simone Weil argues is critical to our spiritual health[224]. In the case of Ravolox, rootedness may be seen in the lives of the Underground Dwellers and the Tribe of the Free. In the first, it comes from an enforced survivalism, where time and space have been telescoped into a single chamber of metal and plastic. In the second, it arises from agricultural tradition, a mainspring for rootedness in human societies for millennia.

The ways in which dwelling can be mapped out in 'The Mysterious Planet' risk missing a crucial point: it is as much a mental state as it is a physical one, weaved and warped in a latticework of experiential threads, which at bottom houses an inimitable and qualitative first-person perception of place. Ravolox, a mystery world, is an

---

[222] Scannell, Leila and Gifford, Robert, 'Defining Place Attachment: A Tripartite Organizing Framework', *Journal of Environmental* Psychology, 30, pp2-3.
[223] Heidegger, *Poetry, Language, Thought*, p159.
[224] Weil, *The Need for Roots*, p40.

expression of the compass of dwelling; its concealed identity inspiring topophilic and topophobic reactions, whilst its enduring human communities, though limited in size and scope, present diverse and complex understandings of locatedness.

The complexity of dwelling, with its capacity to range across philosophical and practical matters, encourages us to consider a somewhat gentler, less perplexing framing, which embraces a more intentional reference to place and placeness. The term 'placehood' may be suitable here, denoting a psycho-physical condition, not unlike childhood and adulthood, which incorporates the qualities contained in dwelling and more clearly points to the concept of place.

Placehood can be used to explore the behaviour of Drathro, who, trapped within its programmed environmental conceptions, is unable to move beyond the rational limits which maintain its survival chamber and keep its human population imprisoned. Thus, Drathro's placehood is as mechanistic and rigid as its metallic body. The term can also be applied to Balazar and Broken Tooth, whose experience of place is predicated on the underground world of the Immortal, and who each join the Tribe of the Free, with its rural setting and concomitant attributes of place.

Placehood for the Doctor and Peri is quite different. Voyaging across the incomprehensible vastness of time and space, to arrive on a seemingly autumnal day on an apparently alien planet, can only extend their understandings of place so far, especially in the case of the well-travelled Doctor. However, where we find nuance here is in their sense of the meaning and value of home. A love of home is summed up in the term oikophilia, from the Ancient Greek word 'oikos' meaning household, and which Roger Scruton sees as a 'family of motives' arising from a 'deep stratum of the human psyche'[225]. Peri's reaction to the true identity of Ravolox, and the Doctor's attempts to help her find perspective in this knowledge, each reveal profound awarenesses of place and corresponding qualities of placehood in human and Time Lord alike.

Interestingly, Scruton's reading of oikophilia directs us 'to live the civic life' by 'creating and sustaining neighbourhoods' and 'imbuing our successors with a spirit of stewardship that we also, in our own actions, display.'[226] In the world that Balazar, Merdeen and their fellow survivors inherit at the close of 'The Mysterious Planet', there is the promise of such a love of home, nourished by the placehood each of them possesses, purchased through the struggle of centuries, to one day reclaim their misplaced planet.

---

[225] Scruton, Roger, *Green Philosophy*, p26.
[226] Scruton, *Green Philosophy*, p413.

BIBLIOGRAPHY

Books

Adams, Richard, *Watership Down*. 1972. England, Penguin Books Ltd, 1978. ISBN 9780140039580.

Agnew, John, *Place and Politics*. 1987. Oxon, Routledge, 2015. ISBN 9780043201770.

Agnew, John and Corbridge, Stuart, *Mastering Space*. 1995. London, Routledge, 2003. ISBN 9780203422380.

Aristotle, *Nicomachean Ethics* (Ηθικὰ Νικομάχεια [Ethika Nikomacheia]). C340 BCE. James Edward Cowell Welldon, trans, New York, Prometheus Books, 1987. ISBN 9780879753788.

Baggini, Julian, *The Ego Trick*. London, Granta, 2011. ISBN 9781847082732.

Baggini, Julian, *How the World Thinks*. 2018. London, Granta Books, 2019. ISBN 9781783782307.

Baker, JA, *The Peregrine*. 1967. London, William Collins, 2017. ISBN 9780008216214.

Beinhocker, Eric D, *The Origin of Wealth*. New York, Random House, 2006. ISBN 9781578517770.

Blackmore, Susan, and Troscianko, Emily T, *Consciousness: An Introduction*. 2004. Third Edition, Oxon, Routledge, 2018. ISBN 9781315755021.

Borsodi, Ralph, *This Ugly Civilization*. New York, Simon and Schuster, Inc, 1929.

Boserup, Ester, *The Conditions of Agricultural Growth: The Economics of Agrarian Change Under Population Pressure.* London, George Allen & Unwin Ltd, 1965.

Boserup, Ester, *Population & Technological Change: A Study of Long-Term Trends.* Chicago, University of Chicago Press, 1981. ISBN 9780226066745.

Bowen, Ann, Day, Andy, Parkinson, Alan, Ellis, Victorian, Hunt, Paul, Kitchen, Rebecca, Kyndt, Claire, Nagle, Garrett, Walshe, Nicola and Young, Helen, *Geography Student Book.* Cambridge, Cambridge University Press, 2016. ISBN 9781316603185.

Camus, Albert, *The Myth of Sisyphus* (*Le Mythe de Sisyphe*). 1942. Justin O'Brien, trans, London, Penguin Books Ltd, 2005. ISBN 9780141023996.

Chalmers, David J, *The Conscious Mind: In Search of a Fundamental Theory.* 1996. Oxford, Oxford University Press, 1997. ISBN 0195117891.

Chalmers, David J, ed, *Philosophy of Mind: Classical and Contemporary Readings.* Oxford, Oxford University Press, 2002. ISBN 9780195145816.

Chalmers, David J, 'Consciousness and Its Place in Nature'.

Cresswell, Tim, *Place: An Introduction.* 2004. West Sussex, John Wiley and Sons Ltd, 2015. ISBN 9780470655627.

De Jonge, Eccy, *Spinoza and Deep Ecology.* 2004. London, Routledge, 2016. ISBN 9780754633273.

Deakin, Roger, *Waterlog.* 1996. London, Vintage, 2000. ISBN 9780099282556.

Descartes, René, *A Discourse on the Method* (*Discours de la Méthode*) 1637. Ian Maclean, trans, Oxford, Oxford University Press, 2006. ISBN 9780192825148.

Diamond, Jared, *Collapse: How Societies Choose to Fail or Succeed*. 2004. New York, Viking Penguin, 2005. ISBN 0670033375.

Fiennes, Peter, *Oak and Ash and Thorn*. London, Oneworld Publications, 2017. ISBN 9781786073211.

Gale, Stephen and Olsson, Gunnar, eds, *Philosophy in Geography*. Holland, D Reidel Publishing Company, 1979.

Tuan, Yi-Fu, 'Space and Place: Humanistic Perspective' pp387-427.

Godfrey-Smith, Peter, *Other Minds: The Octopus and the Evolution of Intelligent Life*. 2017. London, William Collins, 2018. ISBN 9780008226299.

Grahame, Kenneth, *The Wind in the Willows*. 1908. London, Harper Press, 2011. ISBN 9780007902279.

Gray, John, *Straw Dogs: Thoughts on Humans and Other Animals*. 2002. London, Granta Publications, 2003. ISBN 9781862075962.

Hall, Bolton, *Three Acres and Liberty*. 1907. New York, The Macmillan Company, 1918.

Hamer, Marc, *A Life in Nature: Or How to Catch a Mole*. 2019. Great Britain, Vintage, 2020. ISBN 9781784709938.

Hauxwell, Hannah and Cockcroft, Barry, *Seasons of My Life: The Story of a Solitary Daleswoman*. London, Arrow Books Limited, 1990. ISBN 9780099729709.

Heidegger, Martin, *Being and Time* (*Sein und Zeit*). 1927. John Macquarrie and Edward Robinson, trans, Oxford, Blackwell, 2000. ISBN 9780631197706.

Heidegger, Martin, *Poetry, Language, Thought*. 1971. Albert Hofstadter, trans, New York, HarperPerennial ModernClassics, 2001. ISBN 9780060937287.

Heidegger, Martin, *What Is Called Thinking?* (*Was heißt Denken?*). 1954. J Glenn Gray, trans, New York. HarperPerennial, 2004. ISBN 9780060905286.

Hobbes, Thomas, *Leviathan*. 1651. London. J. M. Dent & Sons Ltd, 1914.

Hobbes, Thomas, *The Collected Works of Thomas Hobbes*. 1839-1845. Volume 1. Sir William Molesworth, ed. London. Routledge / Thoemmes Press, 1992. ISBN 9780415088114.

Holden, Edith, *The Country Diary of an Edwardian Lady*. 1977. London, Michael Joseph Ltd / Webb & Bower, 1985. ISBN 9780718115814.

Homer-Dixon, Thomas F, *The Upside of Down: Catastrophe, Creativity, and the Renewal of Civilization*. Washington, DC., Island Press, 2006. ISBN 9781597260657.

Hopkins, Gerard Manley, *Look Up at the Skies! Poems and Prose.* London, Bodley Head, 1972. ISBN 9780370012599.

Hume, David, *A Treatise of Human Nature*. 1739. Lewis Amherst Selby-Bigge, ed, London. Clarendon Press, 1896.

Hunt, Nick, *Where the Wild Winds Are*. 2017. London, Nicholas Brealey Publishing, 2018. ISBN 9781473665750.

Jackson, Frank, *Mind, Method and Conditionals: Selected Essays.* 1998. Oxon, Routledge, 2014. ISBN 9780415165747.

Jenkins, Richard, *Social Identity.* Third Edition. 1996. Oxon, Routledge, 2008. ISBN 9780203927410.

Krasny, Marianne E, *Advancing Environmental Education Practice*. Ithaca NY, Cornell University Press, 2020. ISBN 9781501747083.

Leibniz, Gottfried von, *The Monadology and Other Philosophical Writings* (*La Monadologie*). 1st ed, 1714. Robert Latta, trans, London, Oxford University Press, 1948.

Leopold, Aldo, *A Sand County Almanac*. 1949. Oxford, Oxford University Press, 1989. ISBN 9780195059281.

Locke, John, *An Essay Concerning Human Understanding*. 1689. Pennsylvania State University, Electronic Classics Series, 1999.

Macfarlane, Robert, *The Wild Places*. 2007. London, Granta Publications, 2017. ISBN 9781783784493.

Malthus, Thomas R, *An Essay on the Principle of Population*, vol 1. 6th ed, 1826. Indianapolis, The Online Library of Liberty.

McGinn, Colin, *Problems in Philosophy: The Limits of Inquiry*. Oxford, Blackwell Publishing, 1993. ISBN 9781557864741.

Miller, Walter M, *A Canticle for Leibowitz*. 1959. London, Orbit, 1993. ISBN 9781857230147.

Monbiot, George, 2014. *Feral.* London, Penguin Books. ISBN 9780226205557.

Morgan-Grenville, Roger, *Across A Waking Land*. London, Icon, 2023. ISBN 9781785789762.

Mulhall, Stephen, *Heidegger and Being and Time*. London and New York, Routledge, 1996. ISBN 9780415100939.

Næss, Arne, *There is No Point of No Return*. London, Penguin Books, 2021. ISBN 9780241514610.

Ostrom, Elinor, *Governing the Commons: The Evolution of Institutions for Collective Action*. 1990. Cambridge, Cambridge University Press, 2003. ISBN 9780521405997.

Plato, *The Republic*. (Πολιτεία [Politeia]). C375 BCE. Alexander Dunlop Lindsay, trans, London, JM Dent, 1995. ISBN 9780460873826.

Pretor-Pinney, Gavin, *The Cloudspotter's Guide*. London, Hodder and Stoughton Ltd, 2006. ISBN 9780340895894.

Butler, RJ, ed, *Analytical Philosophy* vol 2. Oxford, Blackwell, 1965.

Putnam, Hilary, 'Brains and Behavior.'

Relph, Edward, *Place and Placelessness*. London, Pion Limited, 1976. ISBN 9780850860559.

Ryle, Gilbert, *The Concept of Mind*. 1949. London, Penguin Books, 2000. ISBN 9780141182179.

Sartre, Jean-Paul, *Being and Nothingness* (*L'Ětre Et Le Néant*). 1943. Hazel E Barnes, trans, London, Routledge, 2000. ISBN 9780415040297.

Schumacher, EF, *Small is Beautiful: Economics as If People Mattered*. 1973. New York, HarperPerennial, 1989. ISBN 9780060916305.

Scruton, Roger, *News from Somewhere*. London, Continuum, 2004. ISBN 9780826490919.

Scruton, Roger, *Green Philosophy*. 2012. London, Atlantic Books,

2013. ISBN 9781848872028.

Seymour, John, *The Complete Book of Self-Sufficiency*. London, Faber and Faber, 1976. ISBN 9780571110957.

Shepherd, Nan, *The Living Mountain*. 1977. Edinburgh, Canongate Books Ltd, 2011. ISBN 9780857861832.

Terney, Rob, Rizvi, Fazal and Ercikan, Kadriye, eds, *International Encyclopedia of Education* Volume 6. 4th ed. Oxford, Elsevier Publishers, 2023.

Shute, Valerie J, Fulwider, G Curt, Lui, Zhichun and Rahimi, Seyedahmad, 'Machine Learning' pp83-91.

Tivy, Joy and O'Hare, Greg, *Human Impact on the Ecosystem*. 1981. Edinburgh, Oliver and Boyd, 1993. ISBN 9780050032039.

Trigg, Dylan, *Topophobia: A Phenomenology of Anxiety.* 2016. London, Bloomsbury Academic, 2017. ISBN 9781474283229.

Tuan, Yi-Fu, *Topophilia: A Study of Environmental Perception, Attitudes and Values*. 1974. New York, Columbia University Press, 1990. ISBN 9780231073950.

Tuan, Yi-Fu, *Space and Place: The Perspective of Experience*. 1977. Minneapolis MN, University of Minnesota Press, 2001. ISBN 9780816638772.

Verne, Jules, *A Fantasy of Dr Ox* (*Une Fantaisie du Docteur Ox*). 1872. Andrew Brown, trans, UK, Alma Books Ltd, 2019. ISBN 9781847497970.

Weil, Simone, *The Need for Roots* (*L'Enracinement*). 1949. Arthur Wills, trans, London, Routledge, 2005. ISBN 9780415271028.

Periodicals

Bachmetjevas, Viktoras, 'Imaginary Construction and Lessons in Living Forward'. *History of European Ideas*, 47(3), pp470-83, 2021.

Boserup, Ester, 'The Impact of Scarcity and Plenty on Development'. *The Journal of Interdisciplinary History*, 14(2), pp383-407, 1983.

Bowring, Jacky, 'Topophilia and Topophobia in the Post-Earthquake Landscape of Christchurch, New Zealand'. *Revista Geográfica del Sur* 4(6), pp103-22, 2013.

Brace, Pedro, 'A Simple Woodland Life'. *Reforesting Scotland*, (45), pp16-17, 2012.

Churchland, Paul M, 'Reduction, Qualia, and the Direct Introspection of Brain States'. *The Journal of Philosophy*, 82(1), pp8-28, 1985.

Cleeremans, Axel, 'The Radical Plasticity Thesis: How the Brain Learns to be Conscious'. *Frontiers in Psychology* 2, pp1-12, 2011.

Cuba, Lee, and Hummon, David, 'A Place to Call Home: Identification with Dwelling, Community, and Region'. *The Sociological Quarterly*, 34(1), pp111-31, 1993.

Czemiel, Grzegorz, ''Brought up to Live Double Lives': Intelligence and Espionage as Literary and Philosophical Figures in Ciaran Carson's *Exchange Place* and *For All We Know*'. *Text Matters: A Journal of Literature, Theory and Culture*, 11, pp35-50, 2021.

Deng, Jianyang. and Lin, Yijia, 'The Benefits and Challenges of ChatGPT: An Overview'. *Frontiers in Computing and Intelligent Systems*, 2(2), pp81-83, 2023.

Fermor, John, And Steele, John M, 'The design of Babylonian

Waterclocks: Astronomical and Experimental Evidence'. *Centaurus*, 42(3), pp210-22, 2000.

Gare, Arran, 'Internalizing Aldo Leopold's Land Ethic'. *Cosmos and History: The Journal of Natural and Social Philosophy*, 17(3), pp397-420, 2021.

Gaspar de Freitas, Joana, 'Landscapes of Fear: the Portuguese Coast'. *The Nautilus*, VIII, pp27-59, 2016.

Giles, James, 'The No-Self Theory: Hume, Buddhism, and Personal Identity'. *Philosophy East and West*, 43(2), pp175-200, 1993.

Halstead, Huw, 'Cyberplace: From Fantasies of Placelessness to Connective Emplacement'. *Memory Studies*, 14(3), pp561-71, 2021.

Hud, Nicholas V, Cafferty, Brian J, Krishnamurthy, Ramanarayanan and Williams, Loren Dean, 'The Origin of RNA and "My Grandfather's Axe"'. *Chemistry & Biology*, 20(4), pp466-74, 2013.

Hull, R Bruce IV, Lam, Mark and Vigo, Gabriela, 'Place Identity: Symbols of Self in the Urban Fabric'. *Landscape and Urban Planning*, 28, pp109-20, 1994.

Issel, William H, 'Ralph Borsodi and the Agrarian Response to Modern America'. *Agricultural History*, 41(2), pp155-66, 1967.

Jackson, Frank, 'Epiphenomenal Qualia'. *The Philosophical Quarterly*, 32(127), pp127-36, 1982.

Jackson, Frank, 'What Mary Didn't Know'. *The Journal of Philosophy*, 83(5), pp291-95, 1986.

Kurzweil, Ray, 'How to Make a Mind', *The Futurist*, March-April 2013, pp14-17.

Martínez de Arbulo, Alejandro, 'The Ship of Theseus: A Misleading Paradox? The Authenticity of wooden built heritage in Japanese Conservation Practice'. *Journal of Architectural Conservation*, 29(2), pp151-67, 2023.

Massey, Doreen, 'A Global Sense of Place'. *Marxism Today*, pp24-29, 1991.

McGinn, Colin, 'Can We Solve the Mind-Body Problem?' *Mind*, New Series, 98(391) pp349-66, 1989.

Libet, Benjamin, Gleason, Curtis A, Wright, Elwood W and Pearl, Dennis K, 'Time of Conscious Intention to Act in Relation to Onset of Cerebral Activity (Readiness-Potential): The Unconscious Initiation of a Freely Voluntary Act'. *Brain*, 106(3), pp623-42, 1983.

Lundborg, Tom, 'Secrecy and Subjectivity: Double Agents and the Dark Underside of the International System'. *International Political Sociology*, 15, pp443-59, 2021.

Næss, Arne, 'The Shallow and the Deep, Long-Range Ecology Movement: A Summary'. *Inquiry: An Interdisciplinary Journal of Philosophy* 16(1-4), pp95-100, 1973.

Nagel, Thomas, 'What Is It Like to Be a Bat?' *The Philosophical Review*, 83(4), pp435-50, 1974.

Nasong'o, Shadrack Wanjala, 'Environmental Policy and Practice in Kenya: Between Cornucopians and Neo-Malthusians'. *The International Journal on Green Growth and Development*, 3(1), pp1-19, 2017.

O'Flynn, Michael, 'Food Crises and the Ghost of Malthus'. *New Proposals: Journal of Marxism and Interdisciplinary Inquiry*, 3(1), pp33-41, 2009.

Peng, Jianchao, Strijker, Dirk and Wu, Qun, 'Place Identity: How Far Have We Come in Exploring Its Meanings?' *Frontiers in Psychology*, 11, pp1-19, 2020.

Polletta, Francesca and Jasper, James M, 'Collective Identity and Social Movements'. *Annual Review of Sociology*, 27, pp283-305, 2001.

Proshansky, Harold M, 'Theoretical Issues in Environmental Psychology'. *The School Review*, 82(4), pp541-55, 1974.

Purbrick, Louise, 'The Dream Machine: Charles Babbage and His Imaginary Computers'. *Journal of Design History* 6(1), pp9-23, 1993.

Qazimi, Shukran, 'Sense of Place and Place Identity'. *European Journal of Social Sciences Education and Research*, 1(1), pp248-52, 2014.

Rambelli, Fabio, 'Floating Signifiers: The Plural Significance of the Grand Shrine of Ise and the Incessant Re-signification of Shinto'. *Japan Review* 27, pp221-42, 2014.

Relph, Edward, 'The Phenomenological Foundations of Geography'. Toronto: Department of Geography, University of Toronto. Discussion Paper No 21, December 1976.

Relph, Edward, 'Digital disorientation and place'. *Memory Studies*, 14(3), pp572-77, 2021.

Scaltsas, Theodore, 'The Ship of Theseus'. *Analysis*, 40(3), 1980.

Scannell, Leila and Gifford, Robert, 'Defining Place Attachment: A Tripartite Organizing Framework'. *Journal of Environmental* Psychology, 30, pp1-10, 2010.

Searle, John R, 'Minds, Brains, and Programs'. *The Behavioural and Brain Sciences* 3, pp417-57, 1980.

Sedley, David, 'The Stoic Criterion of Identity'. *Phronesis*, 27(3), pp255-75, 1982.

Šimáček, Petra, Šerý, Milosav, Fiedor, David and Brisudová, Lucia, 'To Fear or Not to Fear? Exploring the Temporality of Topophobia in Urban Environments'. *Moravian Geographical Reports* 28(4), pp308-21, 2020.

Stets, Jan E and Burke, Peter J, 'Identity Theory and Social Identity Theory'. *Social Psychology Quarterly*, 63(3), pp224-37, 2000.

Strawson, Galen, 'The Impossibility of Moral Responsibility'. *Philosophical Studies*, 75(1-2), pp5-24, 1994.

Tuan, Yi-Fu, 'Place: An Experiential Perspective'. *Geographical Review*, 65(2), pp151-65, 1975.

Turing, Alan, 'Computing Machinery and Intelligence'. *Mind* 49, pp433-60, 1950.

Upton, Patrick, 'Forty Years Living And Learning'. *Reforesting Scotland* (45), pp10-11, 2012.

Wilder, Ursula M, 'The Psychology of Espionage'. *Studies in Intelligence*, 61(2), pp19-36, 2017.

Wilder, Ursula M, 'Odysseus, the Archetypal Spy'. *International Journal of Intelligence and CounterIntelligence*, 34(4), pp799-815, 2021.

Zimmerman, Michael E, 'Rethinking the Heidegger–Deep Ecology Relationship'. *Environmental Ethics*, 15(3), pp195-224, 1993.

Film

Berrow, Joya, and Jane, Lucy, dirs, *Eve: The Off-Grid Life of a Nine-Year-Old Climate Activist*. 2021.

Scott, Ridley, dir, *Blade Runner*. 1982.

Television

Doctor Who. BBC, 1963-.

The Good Life. BBC, 1975-78.

Only Fools and Horses. BBC, 1981-93, 1996, 2003.

Heroes and Villains, 1996.

Survivors. BBC, 1975-77.

Web

[All links accessed 16 May 2025]

Berrow, Joya, and Jane, Lucy, *Eve: The Off-Grid Life of a Nine-Year-Old Climate Activist*. YouTube, 1 June 2021. https://www.youtube.com/watch?v=zSJTDbB3K-U.

Clarke, Peter GH, 'The Libet Experiment and Its Implications for Conscious Will', *Faraday Paper 17*, The Faraday Institute for Science and Religion, St Edmund's College, Cambridge, 2013. https://www.faraday.cam.ac.uk/wp-content/uploads/resources/Faraday%20Papers/Faraday%20Paper%2017%20Clarke_EN.pdf.

England, Kate Arsac, 'How Human Activity Has Changed Earth's Land Surface'. *Earth.Org*, 21 August 2020. https://earth.org/human-activity-land-surface-changes/.

Gunderman, Richard, 'John Keats' Concept of "Negative Capability" – or Sitting in Uncertainty – is Needed Now More Than Ever'. *The Conversation*, 22 February 2021. https://theconversation.com/john-keats-concept-of-negative-capability-or-sitting-in-uncertainty-is-needed-now-more-than-ever-153617.

Hardin, Garrett, 'The Tragedy of the Commons'. *Science*, 162(3859), 1968, pp1243-48. https://iseethics.wordpress.com/wp-content/uploads/2013/02/hardin-garrett-the-tragedy-of-the-commons.pdf.

Harford, Tim, 'What Happens When We're Too Old to Be "Useful"?' *BBC News*, 22 January 2020. https://www.bbc.co.uk/news/business-50673645.

Howard, Sally, 'The Rise of Woodland Off-Gridders: "It Makes More Sense Than a Nine-to-Five"', *The Guardian*, 3 July 2023. https://www.theguardian.com/society/2023/jul/03/the-rise-of-woodland-off-gridders-it-makes-more-sense-than-a-nine-to-five.

Kraut, Richard, 'Aristotle's Ethics'. Zalta, Edward N, ed, *The Stanford Encyclopedia of Philosophy*, summer 2018 edition, 2018. https://plato.stanford.edu/archives/sum2018/entries/aristotle-ethics/.

Ludden, David, 'Can We Have Justice Without Free Will?', *Psychology Today*, 27 July 2020. https://www.psychologytoday.com/gb/blog/talking-apes/202007/can-we-have-justice-without-free-will.

Mahan, *TARDIS Guide*, 'Review of The Mysterious Planet', 14 April 2025. https://tardis.guide/reviews/story-the-mysterious-planet/Mahan/

Marquette, Catherine M, 'Turning but Not Toppling Malthus: Boserupian Theory on Population and the Environment Relationships'. *CMI Working Paper*, WP, 16, 1997. https://www.cmi.no/publications/1158-turning-but-not-toppling-malthus.

Mind, '5 Ways to Wellbeing'. 2025. https://www.mind.org.uk/workplace/mental-health-at-work/five-ways-to-wellbeing/.

Relph, Edward, 'Topophilia and Topophils', 2015. Placeness, Place, Placelessness, 30 October 2015. http://www.placeness.com/2015/10.

Schumacher Centre for New Economics, 'Schumacher on Buddhist Economics'. 1 December 2014. https://www.youtube.com/watch?v=3Eo3k-jCHRo.

Smith, Colin D, 'Who Review: The Mysterious Planet', *www.colindsmith.com*, 1 May 2018. https://www.colindsmith.com/blog/2018/05/01/who-review-the-mysterious-planet/

Thurgill, James, 'A Fear of the Folk: On Topophobia and the Horror of Rural Landscapes', *Revenant*, No 5, March 2020. http://www.revenantjournal.com/wp-content/uploads/2020/03/2-James-Thurgill.pdf.

World Nuclear Association, 'Chernobyl Accident 1986'. 17 February 2025. https://world-nuclear.org/information-library/safety-and-security/safety-of-plants/chernobyl-accident#resettlement-of-contaminated-areas.

ACKNOWLEDGEMENTS

I am immensely grateful to Stuart Douglas, Kara Dennison and Philip Purser-Hallard for their care and precision in transforming a first draft effort into a working manuscript. In particular, I would like to thank Stuart Douglas for his patience and support throughout the process, which began on a winter's day at year's end and continued through a series of email correspondences for almost three years, during which time ideas of place and dwelling began to find focus.

BIOGRAPHY

Jez Strickley has been a teacher for nearly twenty-five years and an occasional writer for almost as long. His credits include a decade as editor of the Canadian **Doctor Who** fan magazine *Whotopia* and guest editor for the **Doctor Who** Appreciation Society's *Celestial Toyroom*. His byline has appeared in a number of publications, including *Vworp Vworp!* and *The Independent Schools Magazine*. When not writing, he enjoys hiking in high places and sunny afternoons reading the books of Robert Macfarlane.